Forts, Fights, and Frontier Sites

Wyoming Historic Locations

Forts, Fights, and Frontier Sites

Wyoming Historic Locations

Candy Moulton

HIGH PLAINS PRESS

The Wyoming bucking horse and rider trademark is federally registered by the State of Wyoming and is licensed for restricted use through the Secretary of State.

The cover illustration, *Frémont Addressing the Indians at Fort Laramie*, is an original antique woodcut by George de Forest Brush from *The Century* magazine, 1891. North Wind Picture Archives.

Library of Congress Cataloging-in-Publication Data
Moulton, Candy Vyvey
  Forts, fights, and frontier sites : Wyoming historic locations / Candy Moulton.
    p. cm.
  Includes bibliographical references and index.
  ISBN 978-0-931271-93-9 (cloth : alk. paper) --
  ISBN 978-0-931271-92-2 (trade paper : alk. paper)
  1. Historic sites--Wyoming--Guidebooks. 2. Wyoming--Guidebooks.
  3. Wyoming--History, Local. I. Title.
  F759.3.M68 2010
  978.7--dc22
                                                    2010015893

HIGH PLAINS PRESS
403 CASSA ROAD
GLENDO, WYOMING 82213
WWW.HIGHPLAINSPRESS.COM
ORDERS & CATALOGS: 1-800-552-7819

FIRST PRINTING
10 9 8 7 6 5 4 3 2 1

Manufactured in the United States of America

READ THIS FIRST

Forts, Fights, and Frontier Sites offers readers a directory of numerous sites that played an important role in the history of Wyoming and the westward expansion and, thus, the history of the United States. The book is not intended as a field guide or roadmap to historic sites; in fact, many of the sites bear no signs of the events that transpired there or the structures that once stood there. Nor is the book all inclusive: not every frontier or military site in Wyoming appears in the book, although those most well known have an entry, as do many that are not as commonly recognized.

Sites related to overland emigration appear, including posts, supply stations, crossings, campsites, and landmarks related to historic trails and routes. It also contains references to places that have a connection to American Indians, the first explorers, military operations, and early westward expansion.

Entries appear alphabetically and specific locations are included for most sites with public access. The icon 〒 appears in the entry of those sites that have a historic marker or an interpretive center.

The key below identifies the icons that accompany these primary site categories:

 Early treks, expeditions, and trapper associations
Military sites
Indian sites
 Trails and routes, including Pony Express and stage
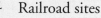 Railroad sites
Natural formations, rivers, creeks, springs, forests
〒 Marker or interpretive center at the site

A Note About Access

It's important to remember that many of the frontier sites have settled back into the landscape, so in many cases all that visitors may see are slight indentations in the land where buildings once stood or perhaps a few dilapidated foundations. Many sites are now on private property, and permission must be obtained to visit them, so please do not visit those places without first contacting landowners.

For assistance in locating sites, or following routes, contact local museums, where you will almost always find people who know them and can tell you whether you can visit them and how to get there.

Terms Used in This Book

Some terms in this book may be used in ways unfamiliar to modern readers. A "station" on the various historic trails was a place where travelers could receive a variety of services. While some were merely a single structure built from logs, sandstone, or other natural material, some stations were well established and had several buildings, including areas for lodging of travelers, and corrals and barns for livestock. Some stations also had services such as food and mail. These more "full service" stations became known as "home stations." Those that had more limited services—perhaps just a change of livestock for stagecoaches or mail riders—were "change," "swing," or "relay" stations. Many of the better established stations also had telegraph services once the transcontinental telegraph was in place in 1861.

In the early period of the fur trappers and traders, a "fort" was a location where those mountain men could exchange pelts for supplies. Not until frontier army operations began in the area did forts have a military connotation. Likewise both the military and nonmilitary enterprises established "camps," which were in most cases more temporary than forts. In the military context, a "cantonment" served as permanent (or in most cases semi-permanent) military stations that had residential areas.

*For wagon master Ben Kern, my trail sister Quackgrass Sally,
and all the great friends I've made traveling by wagon across
Wyoming, particularly Larry and Julie Gomez, Carl Jones, Rod
and Doris Henderson, Chuck and Mary Quillin, Mike and
Carolyn Manley, Vic McDermott, and Donny Marincic.*

ACKNOWLEDGMENTS

I've spent years wandering Wyoming's historical places, making it difficult to list everyone who provided assistance in the research of this book, but I particularly want to say thanks to Dan Neal and the editors (past and present) at the *Casper Star-Tribune*; Dave Perry and Chuck Bowlus, formerly of the *Rawlins Daily Times*; Tamsen Hert in Emmett Chisum Special Collections, University of Wyoming; Chuck Coon; Mike McCrimmon, R. Richard Perue; Lori Van Pelt; the staffs of Wyoming's great museums and historical sites; and the staff members at the Wyoming State Museum, Wyoming State Archives, and Wyoming State Historic Preservation Office.

I am particularly indebted to my good friends Terry Del Bene and James A. Crutchfield, who helped in so many ways, and to University of Wyoming history professor Phil Roberts, who made critical comments on the manuscript. Thank you especially to my family, Steve, Shawn, and Erin Marie.

This book would not have been possible without the pioneering research and writing of historians who have left behind volumes on Wyoming's history. I do appreciate their contributions.

CONTENTS

INTRODUCTION

Two of the most important military sites in Wyoming—Fort Laramie and Fort Bridger—anchor opposite ends of the Oregon–Mormon–California Trails, and both started as fur or outfitting supply posts, not as military posts. Without doubt, the most significant nineteenth century military site in Wyoming is Fort Laramie. It began in 1834 as a fur trade post in a location near the present national historic site, serving fur traders under the name Fort John and later Fort Platte before those locations were abandoned. Strategically located at the confluence of the Laramie River and the North Platte River, Fort Laramie served as a way station for emigrants headed west. In 1849 it became a military post, a distinction that continued until its abandonment in 1890. It also served as the site for several important Indian treaties and became an annuity distribution point for some Plains tribes. Therefore, after 1851 a number of Indians usually camped nearby. Now it is a national historic site that interprets the fur trade and emigrant, Indian, and military history.

Meanwhile, some 375 trail miles farther west, in extreme southwestern Wyoming, Jim Bridger and his partner Louis Vasquez started a trading post in 1842 that became Fort Bridger and served overland travelers for the next decade under Bridger's management. Fort Bridger was then under Mormon control from 1853 until 1857 when the U.S. Army pushed the Mormons back into Utah and formally established Fort Bridger as a military post. The Mormons burned the original Bridger post when they retreated in advance of the army, so the military rebuilt and garrisoned the post until its abandonment in 1890. It now is a Wyoming State Historic Site near the town of Fort Bridger.

Wyoming had no major engagements during the Civil War, although troops stationed at various points along the emigrant trail routes maintained telegraph lines and protected travelers. During that period the military established or operated a number of smaller forts, posts, and stations to serve those troops. The short-lived Pony Express Trail overlapped the emigrant routes with many stations used for the Pony Express, emigrants, and the military at various times.

Just as the Civil War began winding down, Wyoming became a prominent location for military action. The establishment of the Bozeman Trail in 1863, and early travel over it in 1864, set up the first round of battles with American Indians—primarily Lakota, Arapaho, Crow, and Cheyenne warriors. Those early conflicts from 1864 to 1868 became known as the First Sioux War, or Red Cloud's War, because Red Cloud was one of the most influential Lakota war leaders to take part. During that war, which the Indians won, attacks on travelers headed across the Powder River Basin via the Bozeman Trail to gold camps in Montana Territory were routine. The military established three forts along the Bozeman Trail, including two in what became Wyoming Territory (Fort Reno and Fort Phil Kearny) and one in Montana territory (Fort C. F. Smith). But after significant losses to both civilians and to military troops, including the disastrous engagement of December 21, 1866, when Red Cloud and the warriors he led wiped out the entire command of Lieutenant William J. Fetterman, the military withdrew and the Indians burned the forts.

Red Cloud subsequently agreed to a new treaty in 1868, negotiated at Fort Laramie, that reserved the Lakota territory. But the battles were far from over in the region, for there was a second Sioux war, known as Crazy Horse's War, that began in 1874 shortly after Lieutenant Colonel George Armstrong Custer led a reconnaissance mission through the Black Hills where he confirmed the presence of gold. The engagements in that Plains Indian War involved the skirmishes and fights of the Powder River Expedition, including the June 1876 battle at the Rosebud involving troops led by General George Crook, commander of the army's Department of the Platte, and the ultimate Indian victory at the Battle of the Little Bighorn, just north of Wyoming Territory, which resulted in the annihilation of Custer and the men of the Seventh Cavalry under his immediate command. Again it appeared the Indians had won a decisive victory; however, this time the army did not withdraw from the region but instead pursued hostile warriors and their families relentlessly, attacking them in their winter camps.

The Hunkpapa holy man, Sitting Bull, led some of his people safely across the border and into Canada where they remained until 1881. Other Indians involved in the Battle of the Little Bighorn eventually surrendered to troops, including Crazy Horse and his band, who gave themselves up at Hat Creek Station in eastern Wyoming Territory in 1877. They already knew that Cheyenne Dull Knife's village had been attacked and destroyed in a winter raid led by Ranald Mackenzie. Crazy Horse was taken to Fort Robinson, Nebraska, where he was stabbed and killed in September of 1877.

By the time Wyoming became a state in 1890, the Lakota, Cheyenne, Crow, Ute, and Bannock tribal members had been moved to reservations elsewhere. Only the Shoshone and Northern Arapaho tribes, who were traditional enemies, remained in the state, living on the Wind River Indian Reservation in central Wyoming. Chief Washakie of the Shoshones had been given the reservation in the 1860s; under pressure, he later shared it with the Arapahos.

Sites of the key engagements of the so-called Indian Wars appear in the book as do sites related to all aspects of the westward expansion, including early exploration, overland emigration, the transcontinental telegraph and railroad, the Pony Express, and stagecoach travel.

Over the years I have been fortunate to visit most of the sites this book includes. The exploration has been challenging, fun, sometimes surprising. I hope you, the reader, will experience some of that in your own discovery of Wyoming's frontier and military sites.

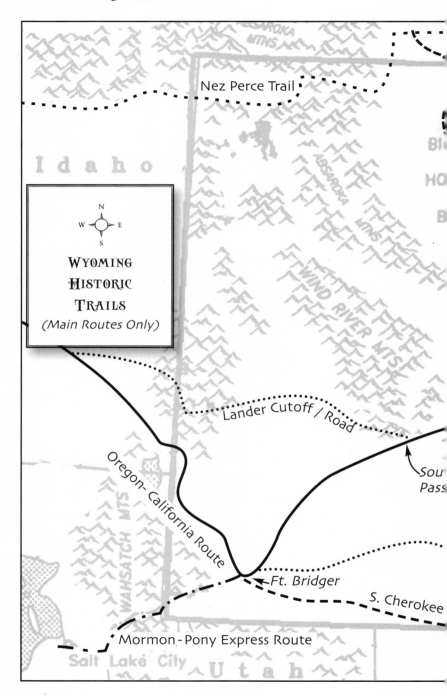

POWDER

RIVER

BLACK
HILLS

BASIN

BIGHORN MTS

Bozeman Trail

Bridger Trail

Cheyenne-
Deadwood Route

Oregon-California-Mormon-
Pony Express Trails

Ft. Laramie

LARAMIE

MEDICINE BOW MTNS

SIERRA MADRE

RANGE

Overland Trail

Colorado

Map adapted from Wyoming Emigrant Trails Map Viewer,
Wyoming State Historic Perservation Office

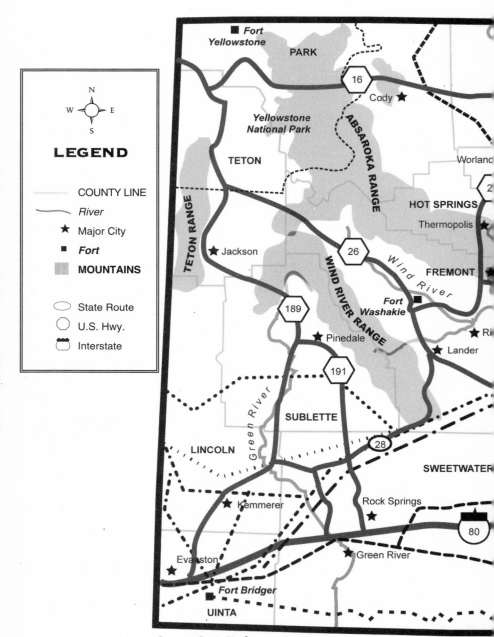

Courtesy Cassie Kraft

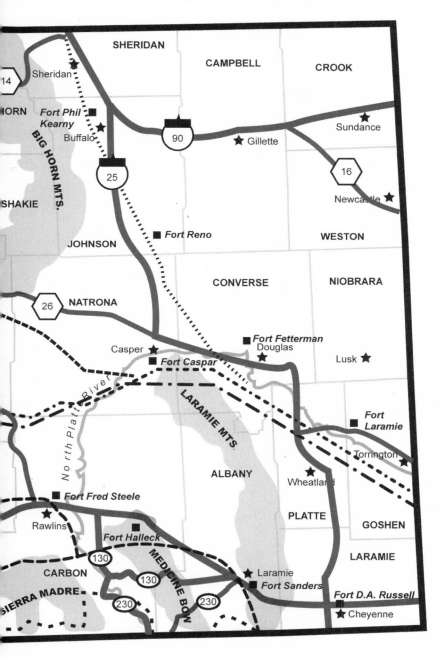

SHERIDAN

CAMPBELL

CROOK

14

Sheridan

Fort Phil
Kearny

Buffalo

90

Gillette

Sundance

16

Newcastle

HORN

SHAKIE

BIG HORN MTS.

JOHNSON

25

Fort Reno

WESTON

NATRONA

26

CONVERSE

NIOBRARA

Casper

Fort Caspar

Fort Fetterman
Douglas

Lusk

North Platte River

LARAMIE MTS.

Fort
Laramie

Torrington

Fort Fred Steele

ALBANY

Wheatland

Rawlins

Fort Halleck

130

130

MEDICINE BOW

PLATTE

GOSHEN

LARAMIE

CARBON

SIERRA MADRE

230

230

Laramie
Fort Sanders

Fort D.A. Russell

Cheyenne

Trail Designations

•–•–•–• Oregon-California-Mormon Trail
ı ı ı ı ı ı ı ı ı Oregon (Sublette Cutoff) Trail
•••••••• Oregon (Lander Cutoff) Trail
–•–•–• Pony Express Trail

ııııııııııı Bozeman Trail
■–■–■–■ Bridger Trail
–––––– Overland-Cherokee Trail
■ ■ ■ ■ ■ Cherokee Trail (South Branch)

Wyoming Historic Locations A-Y

Almond Station
Sweetwater County
Almond Station is another name for the Point of Rocks Station on the
Overland Trail, located just south of Interstate 80 at Point of Rocks.
(*See* Overland Trail.)

Ames Monument
Albany County
In 1882, a large rock monument designed by noted architect Henry
Hobson Richardson was placed at the site of the highest point on
the Union Pacific Railroad route. Named for railroad promoters and
brothers Oliver and Oakes Ames, the Ames Monument is sixty feet
square at the base and sixty feet high with relief medallions of the
brothers, sculpted by famed artist Augustus Saint-Gaudens, mounted in the granite. The monument is about six hundred yards from
the original Union Pacific roadbed. To reach the site, take exit 329
off Interstate 80 and follow the access road.

Aspen Station
Uinta County
This Pony Express relay station is also known as Spring Station or
Quaking Asp Springs Station. (*See* Pony Express Trail.)

Astorian Camp
Natrona County
At a place about five miles west of Devil's Gate, which is located
near Wyoming Highway 220 midway between Casper and Rawlins,

19

Astorians led by Robert Stuart camped in 1812. Their trip was a return journey to the East after having spent the previous year traveling west and establishing a fur trade post at Astoria, Oregon (*see next entry*). The first white men known to camp in this area of Wyoming, they are noted particularly for their "discovery" of the game and Indian trails that would eventually become the migration corridor of hundreds of thousands of people headed to Oregon, California, and Utah over the the California and Oregon Trail.

Astorian Route 🛒 🛶
Bighorn, Washakie, Fremont, Teton, and Sublette Counties

Soon after forming the Pacific Fur Company in 1810, native New Yorker Wilson Price Hunt developed a plan to extend fur trade operations west. He organized two ventures: one involved an ocean expedition of the *Tonquin*, which would sail around the tip of South America to Astoria, Oregon. The other, which he would lead, involved an overland expedition in 1811 that would cross northwest Wyoming, also eventually reaching Astoria, Oregon. The objective of both the ocean crossing and the overland parties was to establish fur trade operations in the Pacific Northwest.

With Scottish-Canadian fur trader Donald Mackenzie, Hunt first traveled to Canada to hire French-Canadian voyageurs and trappers who were familiar with the region. From there Hunt continued eastward to St. Louis before ascending the Missouri River to a wintering point some fifteen miles upstream from St. Joseph, Missouri.

When the westbound trip got underway in the spring of 1811, the Astorian party was joined by trappers John Hoback, Edward Robinson, and Jacob Reznor, who had wintered with Andrew Henry of the Missouri Fur Company on Henry's Fork of Snake River in Idaho. These men knew a route over Wyoming's Big Horn Mountains, Togwotee Pass, and the region that would become known as Jackson's Hole, so although Hunt had intended to follow the route Meriwether Lewis and William Clark had taken in 1804–1806, with his new companions he opted for a more southerly route across Wyoming and south-central Idaho.

The overland party, which comprised fifty-five men—plus interpreter Pierre Dorion, Jr., his wife, Marie, and their two little boys,

Jean Baptiste, aged five, and Jean, aged two—and eighty-two horses, embarked from the Missouri in July 1811 headed toward the Pacific Coast where they would establish Astoria. Once across Wyoming's Big Horns, they trailed through the Wind River Valley and took a route over the Wind River Mountains that became known as Union Pass. From this pass northwest of present Dubois, they spied the jagged mountain range Hunt called the Pilot Knobs. The French Canadian trappers dubbed them Les Trois Tetons; today they are the Grand Tetons.

The explorers then detoured south through the Bondurant Valley to the upper end of the Green River, north of present Pinedale, Wyoming, where they camped, hunted on Horse Creek Meadows, and preserved large quantities of buffalo meat. They again turned north, eventually striking the Snake River and passing through what later became the Hoback Basin and the rugged Hoback Canyon, named for John Hoback due to his early presence in the area.

At what would become Astoria Springs (located off U. S. 189/191 south of Hoback Junction), the party began harvesting cottonwoods for canoes, and Hunt sent John Reed, John Day, and Pierre Dorion on down the Snake River to determine whether it was navigable with dugouts. After a two-day reconnaissance, Reed returned and informed Hunt the route was impassable for canoes or horses, and the river soon had a new name: Mad River.

Hunt followed the Snake River downstream and then, with Indian guides, forded the Snake River, followed a well-traveled Indian trail along Fall Creek, crossed Teton Pass, and dropped into Pierre's Hole (in Idaho) before traveling on to Fort Henry on the North Fork of the Snake River.

The Astorians continued west along the Snake and Columbia Rivers, established Fort Astoria near the Pacific Ocean, and began fur trading. The following year, several of the men, led by Robert Stuart, returned overland to the East, again crossing through Wyoming. Their eastbound journey was relatively uneventful, although it had lasting implications for overland travel through the men's discovery of a route that hundreds of thousands of emigrants headed to Oregon Country, California, and the Mormon settlements in Utah would eventually follow.

Baker Cabin 🕈 ⛵
Carbon County

Jim Baker trapped and roamed throughout Wyoming and Colorado in the early- to mid-nineteenth century but eventually settled in the Little Snake River Valley where he built a sturdy cabin. No longer on its original site (for a time the cabin was in Cheyenne), the cabin is now on the grounds of the Little Snake River Museum in Savery. The solid wood structure has portholes for firing guns at enemy raiders. The interior now contains photos of Baker.

Bannock Indian Trail Å
Yellowstone National Park

Extending across Yellowstone National Park, the Bannock Indian Trail linked Henry's Lake (in Idaho) with the Mammoth Hot Springs area of Yellowstone across the mountains of the Gallatin Range. The trail then connected with another Indian and game trail that traversed the Gardner River Valley. The route followed the Gardner River to a ford above Tower Falls, then it struck across the Lamar River to near Soda Butte, where it turned eastward to the Clark's Fork and Shoshone Rivers. The trail then continued east into the Bighorn Basin. Bannocks and other Indians used this trail routinely when migrating between summer and winter camps or while on hunting and foraging expeditions.

Barrel Springs Station 🚚
Sweetwater County

Also called Dug Springs Station, this station on the Overland Trail was located in Middle Barrel Springs Canyon. (*See* Overland Trail.)

Bates Battle ▀ Å
Hot Springs County

The Bates Battle took place July 14, 1874, during which some Shoshone Indians served as scouts for the U. S. Army. The battle site was at the head of Nowood Creek about thirty-three miles north of the present town of Moneta. The incident started with a coalition of Lakota, Cheyenne, and Arapaho warriors who crossed into Shoshone territory on the west side of the Big Horn Mountains. After disagreement over whether the intended incursion was to capture horses or to simply raid, the Arapahos pulled out.

Meanwhile, because the enemy tribes had moved onto the Shoshone reservation, Captain Alfred Bates organized a cavalry troop of sixty men at Fort Brown. Those troops joined thirty Shoshones as they rode in search of the Arapaho camp, which they found on Nowood Creek. In the battle that took place between the troops and their Shoshone allies with the Arapahos, most of the Arapaho horses were captured, and fighters from both sides died. Meanwhile, the Lakota and Cheyenne warriors had continued south, eventually making it to near Fort Brown, but they withdrew before making any attack on soldiers or the Shoshones.

Battle Creek/Lake/Mountain 𓏢 🌲 ⛺ 🛶
Carbon County
These sites, located in the Sierra Madre Range of south-central Wyoming and all accessible or visible off of Wyoming Highway 70, get their names from an attack by Indians on trappers in August 1841. A National Forest campground is now located along Battle Creek. (*See* Little Snake River, Indian attack.)

Bear River Station 🚬
Uinta County
This relay station was on the Pony Express trail. (*See* Pony Express Trail.)

Beaver Creek 🌲 🛶
Carbon County
Lieutenant John C. Frémont called this stream, located ten miles east of Encampment, Beaver Dam creek when he camped here on June 14, 1844:

> . . . in the evening encamped on a pretty stream, where there were several beaver dams, and many trees recently cut down by the beaver. We gave to this the name of Beaver Dam creek, as now they are becoming sufficiently rare to

distinguish by their name the streams on which they are found (Frémont 1845, 282).

The area later had two small communities, Downington and Collins, developed by homesteaders and serving as post offices. Both had been deserted by the 1920s as transportation improvements made it easier for residents in the area to conduct shopping and trade in Encampment or even Saratoga.

Bed Tick Station 🚬
Converse County
Located about five miles southwest of present Douglas, Bed Tick Station served the Pony Express and also was a stage station. (*See* Pony Express Trail.)

Bennett's Ferry 🚬
Carbon County
The Overland Trail crossed the North Platte River about a dozen miles north of Saratoga at Bennett's Ferry. With a partner named Redup, Edward Wakeman Bennett began operating a store and ferry business at the North Platte Crossing in November 1866. The ferry functioned by means of a system of cables that were strung across the river and anchored by supports on either bank. The ferry itself was a flatboat apparatus that could be maneuvered from one side of the river to the other. High water the following spring destroyed that first venture by Bennett by washing away the ferry support system on either side of the river, so he relocated about two and a half miles up the river and began operating his "Bennett's Ferry" in partnership with Louis Reidsell and Frank Earnest. They had some help from Napoleon Bonaparte "Boney" Earnest, as well. As Boney Earnest writes, "We'd take two wagons west and bring back two agoing east and we caught'em agoing and acoming" (Alcorn 1984, 52). The cost for the ferry was $5.

As he developed his property and business enterprise, Bennett added a blacksmith shop. There is an emigrant-era graveyard beneath the cliffs above the river near the ferry site. The site is now private land and has no general public access. (*See* Overland Trail.)

Benton 🚂
Carbon County

This end-of-tracks, or hell-on-wheels, town named for Missouri Senator Thomas Hart Benton, a proponent of a transcontinental rail service, grew with the building of the Union Pacific Railroad across southern Wyoming in 1868. Its precursor was Brownsville, located on the land later set aside for military use at Fort Fred Steele. When the military post was under construction, Commander Richard I. Dodge ordered the residents of Brownsville to relocate and make way for the troops. They moved three miles west and established Benton, which was "the meanest place I have ever been in," according to Union Pacific crew boss Jack Casement (1868).

The town soon had five dance halls and twenty-five saloons to serve the patrons, who included workers on the Union Pacific line and camp followers. When sale of liquor was banned in November 1868 (in "company" towns, the decision to limit sales of alcohol came from railroad officials), Benton residents and business proprietors picked up their goods and moved west to Rawlins Springs.

End-of-track towns sprang up all along the Union Pacific Railroad line, in place and booming one day, many of them deserted the next as the tracks pushed west and the residents looked for better opportunity. Because most structures in these communities were temporary—often built of basic frames covered with canvas—they were easily dismantled and taken to the next end-of-tracks town. The towns had no real law and order other than that provided by the bosses on the railroad construction crew.

Big Bend Station 🚃
Sweetwater County

This station on the Overland Trail also served the Pony Express. (*See* Overland Trail.)

Big Laramie Station 🚃
Albany County

Tom Alsop managed this station on the Overland Trail located on the Laramie River about eight miles southwest (upstream) of present

Laramie. The station had a barn, two log buildings used for living areas for Alsop and other company employees and travelers, and a log blacksmith shop. It is now located on private ranch land. (*See* Overland Trail.)

Big Pond Station 🚂
Sweetwater County

This was a swing station, where horse teams were exchanged but only temporary stops made, on the Overland Trail located on Bitter Creek. There is a report of Indians burning the station on July 20, 1867, although such efforts would have had limited effect because the main portion of the structures was built of sandstone and limestone slabs (Erb, Brown & Hughes 1989). A unique aspect of the construction material was the presence of fossilized freshwater shells embedded in the limestone and sandstone (Hurd 1961). (*See also* Overland Trail.)

Big Sandy Station 🚂
Sweetwater County

One of the stage and Pony Express stations, Big Sandy Station was in use from April 1860 until October 1861. The station was located on Big Sandy Creek west of present Farson. At the time explorer and ethnographer Sir Richard F. Burton traveled the route by stage in 1860, a young Mormon couple ran the station. Burton writes:

> We halted for an hour to rest and dine, the people of the station . . . were both English, and of course Mormons they had but lately become tenants of the ranch, but already they were thinking . . . of making their surroundings 'nice and tidy' (1862; reprint 1990, 167).

Big Timber Station 🚂
Sweetwater County

This log trading post located about seventeen miles southwest of present Farson served traffic on the Oregon Trail at the point where it branched three ways into the main trail, the Slate Creek-Kenney route, and the route to the lower crossing of the Green River.

Travelers selected their route based on their intended final destination and how quickly they wanted to reach it. (*See* Parting of the Ways.)

Bisonette's Ferry
Converse County
Joseph Bisonette established a ferry across the North Platte River in the vicinity of Deer Creek in 1849. It also operated during 1850, serving travelers on the Oregon–California Trail. Built from a half dozen or so dugout canoes, the ferry had timbers to form a base or floor so it could transport wagons over the river. People provided the main power by using oars to propel the ferry. A tow line across the river could also be used to pull the ferry forward by hand.

Bitter Cottonwood Stage Station
Platte County
Used as a Pony Express station, Bitter Cottonwood also served as a stage station sometimes called Cottonwood Station. It was located northwest of Guernsey. (*See* Pony Express Trail.)

Bitter Creek Stage Station
Sweetwater County
This station served the Overland Trail and became a railroad grading camp in 1868. (*See* Overland Trail.)

Black Butte Station
Sweetwater County
This station on the Overland Trail likely had a main station built of sandstone and limestone with a pole and dirt roof, plus possibly a powder house. The site, with crumbling walls, is now on lands mined by the Black Butte Coal Company. (*See* Overland Trail.)

Black Hills Expedition, 1875
Laramie, Goshen, Niobrara, and Weston Counties
In May of 1875, the Black Hills Expedition was organized at Fort Laramie under the leadership of Walter P. Jenney and Henry Newton, both from the Columbia School of Mines in New York, and astronomer Horace P. Tuttle of the Cambridge Observatory in Massachusetts

(McGillycuddy 1941). Colonel Richard I. Dodge commanded its military escort.

The seventeen member expedition also had a naturalist, a photographer, a cartographer, a head miner, and ten laborers, all of them under auspices of the Office of Indian Affairs, but it became a joint expedition with the Department of War by virtue of its military escort comprising six companies of the Second and Third Cavalry all under Colonel Dodge's command (Kime 1996).

In a letter to Walter Camp, January 14, 1913, expedition topographer Valentine T. McGillycuddy describes the purpose of the expedition as:

> . . . an independent survey or exploration ordered by Gen. [Ulysses S.] Grant to settle the disputed point as to whether gold existed in the Black Hills in paying quantities. Gen. Custer in his expedition of 1874 having claimed to have so found it while F. V. Hayden in charge of our U. S. Geological Surveys at Washington claimed that he had thoroughly examined this country many years before and that the 'geological formation' was such that gold could not exist in paying quantities" (Reel 1).[1]

The expedition traveled north from Fort Laramie, roughly along the route of what would later become the Cheyenne to Deadwood stage route (and what is now basically U.S. 85). When exploration of the Black Hills got underway, base camps for the expedition were located variously at Jenney Stockade (*see entry*) on Beaver Creek in the western Black Hills near present Newcastle; Camp Harney and Custer City, both along French Creek; and later Camp Crook, south of Rapid Creek all in western Dakota (now South Dakota).

This expedition ultimately established the presence of gold in large quantity in the Black Hills and also prepared some of the earliest maps of the region.

Blair's Stockade
Sweetwater County

In 1866 Overland Trail travelers could get a meal at this trading post near the rock springs that gave the city of Rock Springs its name.

Archibald and Duncan Blair managed the post for the Overland Stage Company, building a corral for livestock that became known as Blair's Stockade. Archibald had come to the West from Scotland during the California gold rush in 1849 and then with brother Duncan relocated to Wyoming where they operated the stage station with the assistance of Becky Thomas, who cooked for travelers. The Blairs later operated a coal mine and sold supplies to the Union Pacific Railroad as the community of Blairtown grew in the area that became Rock Springs. The brothers also had a ranch south of Rock Springs, and eventually both served in the Wyoming Territorial Legislature (Urbanek 1990).

Bone Pile Rifle Pits
Campbell County

Members of the Sawyers Expedition dug these seventeen (some sources say twenty-one) rifle pits August 14, 1865, when they came under attack by Indians. The pits were arranged in a semi-circle and dug along the crest of a knoll overlooking Spring Creek Draw on the northeast. Among the items found at the Bone Pile rifle pits are lead bullets, percussion caps, square nails, and a brass military button. Some of those items are now on display at the Rockpile Museum in Gillette. The rifle pits are located on private land about ten miles southwest of Gillette (Rosenberg 1989). (*See* Sawyers Expedition.)

Bonneville Cabins/Lake/Mountain/Pass
Sublette and Fremont Counties

These sites are named for Captain Benjamin L. E. Bonneville, who explored the area in 1832, eventually establishing Fort Bonneville (*see entry*). He had five cabins at a site in Fremont County that held his trade goods. Major Noyes Baldwin in 1866 used the cabins for trade purposes.

Bordeaux Station
Goshen County

James Bordeaux built a trading post in 1849 at a site about two miles west of present Lingle. The post operated until 1868. For a time it also served as a stage station. Robert Campbell, a traveler on the

Oregon Trail, notes on September 14, 1854, "We traveled 8 miles to Bordeau's Station. There are mountaineers settled here and they do blacksmithing and trade oxen and horses. It was at this place that the Indians killed the 29 soldiers and their officer" (Haines 1981, 118). His mention of soldier deaths refers to the Grattan Massacre (*see entry*). Bordeaux Station also served as a Pony Express relay station.

Box Elder Station 🚂
Converse County
This station, known as U.S. Mail Station No. 27, served the Pony Express and stagecoaches. Its exact location is unknown, but it was about nine miles east of present Glenrock near Box Elder Creek. Explorer Sir Richard Burton arrived here in 1860, writing:

> The station had yet to be built; the whole road was in a transition state at the time of our arrival; there was, however, a new corral for 'forting' against Indians, and a kind of leafy arbor, which the officials had converted into a 'cottage near a wood' (1862; reprint 1990, 135).

Bozeman Trail 🚩 🚂 🏴 ⛺
Converse, Natrona, Johnson, and Sheridan Counties
First used by emigrants from 1864 through 1866 then used as a military road until it was abandoned in 1868 after the Fort Laramie Treaty, the Bozeman Trail is named for a man who pioneered only a fraction of its 600-mile length. Its legacy is one of conflict with some of the Indian tribes through whose territory it crossed.

The September 17, 1851, treaty negotiated with the Indian tribes at Horse Creek near present-day Torrington, Wyoming, established tribal lands. Representatives from the Sioux, Cheyenne, Arapaho, Crow, Arikara, Gros Ventre, Assiniboine, and Mandan tribes agreed to limit hostilities, to make restitution in the event of wrongs committed against emigrants, and to allow roads through their territory. The road they generally agreed to was the major east-west highway of the time—the Oregon–Mormon–California Trail.

The land north of the North Platte River and east of the Big Horn Mountains remained Indian territory—primarily that of the

Sioux, the Arapahos, and the Cheyennes. The Crows ranged farther to the north and west. The area, now known as the Powder River Basin, had abundant grass and game; it was an important part of the tribal territories and certain portions of it were considered sacred.

Prospectors found gold at Bannack, Montana Territory, in the summer of 1862. Then they found gold at nearby Alder Gulch in May 1863, and the rush was on. Knowing the miners from the East would want to reach the gold country as quickly as possible, miner John Bozeman and mountain man John Jacobs left Montana's Beaverhead Valley in early 1863 to find a route that could cut many miles of travel off the trip. Along with Emma, Jacobs' young half-Flathead Indian daughter, they headed east and eventually south along the east flank of the Big Horns. They ran into a party of Indians, who took their food, horses, and other belongings. It was the first of many confrontations that would occur over the life of the trail that earned the title "The Bloody Bozeman."

The Bozeman Trail, during its short history, used a number of differing routes, determined in part by the availability of water and grass, the ease of travel, attempts to find shortcuts, and other factors.

On July 6, 1863, Bozeman and Jacobs, with their guide Rafael Gallegos, led the first wagon train of emigrants onto the Bozeman Trail. They left from Deer Creek on the North Platte River near present Glenrock, Wyoming. Due to Indian hostilities, they did not complete the journey over the trail that year, although Bozeman led a pack train on to Montana after the wagons turned back to return to the Oregon Trail.

In 1864 three wagon trains left from the area of the Richard (Reshaw) Bridge in present Evansville, Wyoming, just east of Casper. They were the first trains to travel the entire trail to Montana's gold fields near Alder Gulch at Virginia City.

On June 16, 1864, Allen Hurlbut led a large wagon train of prospectors from Richard's Bridge up the Bozeman Trail. The Hurlbut train had 124 wagons and 438 people. Hurlbut's train reached Montana after a wagon train of 109 wagons led by John Bozeman, which had departed from Richard's Bridge on June 18, 1864. The Bozeman train reached the Montana gold fields before the Hurlbut train in part because the prospectors with Hurlbut had stopped to prospect in the Big Horn Mountains of north-central Wyoming. Meanwhile, a wagon train organized by John T. Smith left from Richard Bridge a few days after Bozeman's train departed. Later those two parties combined, and they reached Montana together (Badger-Doyle 2001).

Through the next two years, other men led trains of both emigrant and military parties through the region, establishing new routes that are all part of the Bozeman Trail corridor. Jim Bridger, who came west in 1825 as a young man to engage in the fur trade, pioneered more miles of the route than anyone else; yet, his name is on a trail farther to the west. James Sawyers led a military road-building expedition across the area adding to the Bozeman route. (*See also* Sawyers Expedition.)

From the very first explorations by Bozeman and Jacobs until the trail was virtually abandoned as a through-travel route in the late 1860s, there was conflict. Wagon trains often engaged in armed battles with Indians, and many wagon travelers who died in these battles lie buried along the trail.

In 1866 the frontier army established three forts to protect travelers on the trail: Fort Reno and Fort Phil Kearny in what is now Wyoming, and Fort C. F. Smith on the present Crow Indian Reservation in Montana. The Indians protested from the moment the first work to build those forts began. The tribesmen attacked soldiers in some of the bloodiest battles of the Northern Plains during what became known as the First Sioux War, or Red Cloud's War, from 1864 to 1866.

When the confederated tribes succeeded in driving the military from the region in 1867, the Indians immediately burned all three forts, and travel generally ceased over that road to Montana's gold.

Bridger Trail 🚙
Natrona, Washakie, Hot Springs, and Big Horn Counties

Gold seekers looking for a short route to diggings in Alder Gulch, Montana Territory, followed a trail forged by mountain man Jim Bridger that took his name. The Bridger Trail started near the present town of Casper, where travelers left the Oregon–California Trail to head north and west. Used in 1864 and 1865 only, the Bridger

Trail crossed through Bridger's Saddle, went past Lost Cabin and through the Big Horn Basin, exiting the present state of Wyoming near the current town of Frannie. The advantage travelers on the Bridger Trail had over those headed to Montana over the Bozeman Trail was less opposition from Indian tribes for the route west of the Big Horn Mountains and the Powder River Basin. However, the route was through an area that had few creeks and streams so travelers had difficulty locating adequate water for people and livestock.

Bridger–Fraeb Trading Post
Sweetwater County
In 1841 Henry Fraeb joined Jim Bridger to construct a trading post at a location likely about eighteen miles northeast of present Granger. Though Fraeb, a mountain man like Bridger, died in battle with Indians near the Little Snake River that same year (*see* Little Snake River, Indian Attack), Bridger continued to operate their post until 1842, when he relocated to Black's Fork. There with new partner and fellow former trapper Louis Vasquez, Bridger built a post where he knew emigrants would pass. That site became Fort Bridger and was the second provisioning point in present Wyoming for early Oregon-bound travelers. The first place emigrants could get any assistance or supplies was at Fort Laramie, 375 trail miles to the east.

Bridger–Vazquez Trading Post
Uinta County
This trading post, the forerunner to Fort Bridger, was established in 1841 on the Black's Fork of the Green River by Jim Bridger and Louis Vasquez.

Bridger's Ferry
Converse County
Jim Bridger operated a ferry over the North Platte River to serve traffic on the Bozeman Trail from 1864 to 1866. Indians did not bother the ferries along the main east-west trail route as they did travelers farther north in the Powder River Basin of northeast Wyoming. The ferry crossing was near Orin where U.S. Highway 26/87 crosses the North Platte River.

Bridger's Pass/Station 🚚
Carbon County

This was a site on the Overland and Cherokee Trails and the location of a two-room log station on the freight and stage route, about a half mile from the main Overland Trail. It was in use from 1862 until 1865, when travelers reported it had been burned by Indians. It is named for mountain man Jim Bridger, one of the first white men to travel through the area as he forged a route across present southern Wyoming to Great Salt Lake City.

Early day resident Robert Foote built this station and one at Pine Grove. He later said:

> As to the materials that the stations were built of, it was logs: no fancy work about the stations what ever; they were very plain. The buildings were about twenty-five by sixty feet, and they had rooms for passengers to eat, and rooms for forage on one side—plain log buildings (U. S. Congress 1890, as quoted in Alcorn 1984, 28).

Bunsen Peak 🌲 🛶
Yellowstone National Park

The geologic survey of Yellowstone National Park in 1872 included among the team members chemist and physicist Robert W. Bunsen, who later developed the Bunsen burner, and for whom this peak is named.

Burnt Ranch 🍽 🚚
Fremont County

Located on the Oregon Trail in the Upper Sweetwater area, this site gets its name because it was burned shortly after construction. It was one of a series of stations established in 1857 by Hiram Kimball and the Church of Jesus Christ of Latter-day Saints (the Mormons) a few hundred yards from the ninth crossing of the Sweetwater. That Sweetwater crossing, also called Gilbert's Ranch, was one of the zero base points Frederick West Lander used in 1858 as he engineered the Lander Road (*see entry*). A station near Burnt Ranch was part of a mail route Mormon leader Brigham Young established. That station, located adjacent to the Seminoe Cutoff of the Oregon Trail south of the Sweetwater River, was burned by the Mormons in 1857 as they retreated before Colonel Albert Sidney Johnston's pursuing federal troops during the Utah War (*see* Utah War of 1857).

Burnt Ranch was also used for a station serving the Pony Express, the transcontinental telegraph, and then the Overland Stage Line operated by Ben Holladay before he relocated service farther south to the Overland Trail. The shift in Holladay's operations came because of Indian raids on the Oregon Trail route. Burnt Ranch had many names, including Gilbert's Station, Upper Sweetwater Station, and South Pass Station. Between 1862 and 1868, the station was garrisoned by the Eleventh Ohio Volunteers protecting the emigrant trail travelers and the telegraph line. Indians burned the station shortly after it was abandoned. Though the station was later rebuilt, Indians again burned the site, giving it the enduring name of Burnt Ranch. The site is now private property.

Burntfork, Mountain Man Rendezvous, 1825
Sweetwater County

The first trade rendezvous for mountain men took place not far from the site of the present tiny community of Burntfork in 1825. It was organized by trader William Ashley who brought a caravan of fur trapper supplies to the Henry's Fork of the Green River, exchanging the goods for beaver pelts, or plews, which trappers had gathered during the previous year. Subsequent rendezvous took place throughout the intermountain West during the next fifteen years, including at several locations in Wyoming and others in Utah and Idaho.

Caballo Creek Rifle Pits
Campbell County

On August 17, 1865, members of the Sawyers Expedition dug sixteen rifle pits in a semi-circular pattern on a ridge overlooking Caballo Creek, a tributary of the Belle Fourche River. The rifle pits were dug as a precaution when, as Sawyers writes in his diary, "A few Indians were seen during the day lurking behind the bluffs a mile or so from camp" (Badger-Doyle 2001, 360). (*See also* Sawyers Expedition.)

California Trail 🚃

Goshen, Platte, Converse, Natrona, Carbon, Fremont, Sweetwater, Sublette, Uinta, and Lincoln Counties

Discovery of gold at Sutter's Mill on the American Fork River in California in January 1848 led to the gold rush and a flood of prospectors. The Argonauts took three primary routes to the gold fields: by sea around Cape Horn, by water and land over the Isthmus of Panama, and overland on a route that became the California Trail. In Wyoming, the California Trail was the same general route as the Oregon Trail, though there were cutoff routes in the western part of the present state, including the Sublette Cutoff (*see entry*).

Travel on the trail to California actually started years before the gold discovery, when John Bidwell and John Bartleson crossed the route in 1841. The major overland travel, however, began in 1849 and quickly escalated until 1852, which was a peak year in overland trail travel. Those people headed to California as part of the gold rush generally used mules to pull their wagons, as those draft animals allowed a faster crossing than oxen and were more durable than horses. But not all California-bound overland travelers used wagons. Some traveled in pack trains, and others even walked the route carrying their possessions in back packs.

Camp Augur 🚩 🏴 🛖

Fremont County

Established June 28, 1869, by First Lieutenant Patrick Henry Breslin, Fourth U. S. Infantry, and named for Brigadier General Christopher C. Augur, this camp (also called a fort) served Shoshone Indians on the Wind River Indian Reservation. Its location was at the present town of Lander. This post was never designated a fort but served as a subpost of Fort Bridger. It was reorganized on March 28, 1870, and renamed Camp Brown for Captain Frederick H. Brown, Eighteenth U. S. Infantry. Brown had died December 21, 1866, in the Fetterman Fight (*see entry*). Camp Brown was abandoned in 1871 when a new agency for the Shoshone and Arapaho Indians was opened at Fort Washakie.

Camp P. A. Bettens 🏴
Sheridan County

This temporary camp served six companies of the Ninth U.S. Infantry—a unit of Black men who became known as Buffalo Soldiers—from Fort Robinson, Nebraska, from June through November 1892. Located on Powder River near the present community of Arvada, its role was to maintain peace in the region in the aftermath of the Johnson County Invasion (*see entry*).

Camp Brown 🪧 🏴
Fremont County

Named for Captain Frederick Brown of the Eighteenth U.S. Infantry, who died in the December 21, 1866, Fetterman Fight, this was the camp originally known as Camp Augur. It was also a forerunner to Fort Washakie (*see individual entries*).

Camp Carlin 🪧 🏴 🚂
Laramie County

This military camp served as a supply depot for Fort D. A. Russell, established in 1867. Officially Camp Carlin was known as Cheyenne Depot. The first troops stationed there were from the Thirtieth U.S. Infantry and the Second U.S. Cavalry under command of General John D. Stevenson. The primary role of the troops was to provide protection for workers building the transcontinental railroad. In providing troops for protection as well as serving as a supply depot, Camp Carlin was soon the scene for one hundred freight wagons and some fifteen hundred mule teams needed to transport goods to construction workers. The camp had shops for carpenters, harness makers, blacksmiths, and wheelwrights with corrals and stables for the livestock. The wooden buildings also included wagon sheds, cook shacks, bunkhouses, and a commissary. The post remained in operation until 1890. It was located near what is now F. E. Warren Air Force base. (*See also* Fort D. A. Russell.)

Camp Connor 🚩 🚂
Johnson County

This camp, named for General P. E. Connor, was later renamed Fort Reno. (*See* Fort Reno.)

Camp Davis 🚂
Natrona County

Located near the Richard Bridge in present Evansville, this camp was established in 1855. It was renamed Camp Payne in 1858 and later became Post at Platte Bridge (*see also individual entries*).

Camp O. O. Howard 🚂 🚂
Laramie County

This camp, established to provide protection for Union Pacific track-layers and named for General Oliver Otis Howard, Union commander of the Eleventh Corps during the battle at Chancellorsville and later director of the Freedman's Bureau, was located near present Pine Bluffs. Howard is most remembered for his 1877 military campaign to force Nez Perce Indians onto a reservation in Idaho. When the Indians, led by Chief Joseph, Whitebird, Looking Glass, and others, fled Idaho, Howard commanded the troops that pursued them along a 1500-mile trail that crossed Idaho, Montana, Yellowstone National Park, and extreme northern Park County in Wyoming. Chief Joseph eventually surrendered to General Howard and Lieutenant Colonel Nelson Miles at the Bear's Paw Battlefield in northern Montana, just forty miles from Canada, where they would have found refuge.

Camp Marshall 🚂
Converse County

William Henry Jackson, who became known for his early photographs and paintings of the West, found this temporary military post on the west side of LaBonte Creek south of present Douglas abandoned when he passed the area on August 10, 1866. Despite Jackson's reference to the site as "ruins of old Fort LaBonte" (Jackson 1940, 125), the post was never a recognized fort.

Camp McGraw
Fremont County

This "camp" was actually a house named for Lander Road engineer William M. McGraw. The first residents were surveyors from Fort Kearny, Nebraska, who spent the winter of 1857–1858 in the area near present Atlantic City. That survey crew and McGraw assisted in initial planning and work on the Lander Road (*see entry*).

Camp Payne
Natrona County

First established in 1855 and known as Camp Davis, this site in present Evansville was renamed Camp Payne in 1858 but later became officially known as Post at Platte Bridge (*see also individual entries*).

Camp Pilot Butte
Sweetwater County

The U. S. Army established and garrisoned this camp in 1885 in the aftermath of the Chinese Massacre at Rock Springs (*See* Rock Springs, Chinese Massacre, 1885). The site, also known as Camp Rock Springs, was located on five and a half acres of Union Pacific land in a location now bounded on the west by Soulsby Street, on the east by Pilot Butte Avenue, on the north by Bridger Avenue, and on the south by Elias Avenue. The rectangular parade ground on the west side of the camp had two, one-story frame houses for officers. At the opposite side of the parade ground were barracks for enlisted men.

Other structures at the post were a hospital, commissary, canteen, bakery, beer cellar, ice house, barber shop, sergeants' day room, school house, guard house, gun shed, carpenter shop, and wagon shed as well as chicken houses, stables, and corrals. The troops were in place to quell any potential for further violence at the mine. The post was abandoned on March 3, 1899. From then until 1950, the Union Pacific Coal Company used the buildings as dwellings for workers, including foremen and their families who used the former officer quarters.

The Catholic Church obtained the property in 1950 and ultimately operated parochial schools on the site, although by then only one building remained from the period when it had served Camp Pilot Butte.

Camp Scott 📧
Uinta County

Named for General Winfield Scott, a career officer who took part in the War of 1812 and the Mexican-American War and commanded the bodyguard for the inauguration of President Abraham Lincoln, this camp near the site of present Fort Bridger served as a winter camp in 1857 for troops led by Colonel Albert Sidney Johnston taking part in the so-called Utah War. (*See* Utah War of 1857.)

Camp Sheridan 📧
Yellowstone National Park

(*See* Fort Yellowstone.)

Camp Stambaugh 📧 𝖠
Fremont County

Established August 20, 1870, in Smith's Gulch not far from the Oregon Trail and the present community of Atlantic City, this camp came into existence because of threats to gold miners from Indians in the region. It was named for Lieutenant Charles B. Stambaugh, Second U. S. Cavalry, who was killed in a battle with Indians May 4, 1870, in the vicinity of nearby Miner's Delight. Camp Stambaugh had four log barracks for two infantry companies. No longer needed as the threat from Indians diminished, the camp was abandoned on August 17, 1878.

Camp Walbach 📧
Laramie County

Located on South Lodgepole Creek about twenty miles northwest of present Cheyenne, this post was officially a camp and never designated a fort. It was established September 20, 1858, and named for Colonel John De Barth Walbach, who had commanded the Fourth U. S. Artillery at the time of his death on June 10, 1857.

Major Thomas Williams commanded Companies L and M, Fourth U. S. Artillery, as the troops with heavy wagons and about forty head of cattle traveled from Fort Laramie southeast to Cheyenne Pass, where they established Camp Walbach in September 1858 (Ryan 1963). The dual mission of Camp Walbach was guarding the road under construction from Fort Riley, Kansas, to Bridger Pass in south-central Wyoming (which at that time was part of Nebraska Territory), and protecting the supply line for materials transported to the U. S. Army under command of Colonel Albert Sidney Johnston then marching toward Utah in the Utah War (see also Utah War of 1857).

A camp of tents, Walbach accommodations were reinforced with slabs of sandstone three to twelve inches thick that were placed against the bottom edges of the tents. In a September 23, 1858, letter to the Acting Assistant Adjutant General, Major Williams writes:

> These sandstone walls, which reached the height of several feet, served the double object of shelter and defence [*sic*], according the tents' occupants some degree of protection from the weather and also from possible Indian attacks (Williams 1858).

The camp had a hospital that, according to post medical reports, treated soldiers for a variety of ailments, largely caused as result of a poor diet comprising bacon, hard bread, and coffee, supplemented with salt, sugar, and vinegar; the latter was necessary to prevent scurvy in men whose diet included little or no fruit and vegetables.

Camp Walbach had a garrison of ninety-three enlisted men and six officers in September 1858, which may have been the peak of activity. On March 23, 1859, the camp received orders calling for its abandonment. The same orders also called for abandonment of the "fort" at Platte Bridge (Ryan 1963). Camp Walbach was subsequently abandoned on April 19, 1859.

Camp Winfield 🏴
Sublette County

Colonel E. B. Alexander established this military camp in 1857 during the Utah, or Mormon, War. It was a forward post—a place where advance troops could station themselves and their supplies as the larger army marched toward their position. Mormon raiders harassed troops at the camp before a raid at Simpson's Hollow in early October of 1857. (*See also* Simpson's Hollow, Mormon's Raid and Utah War of 1857.)

Cantonment Reno 🏴
Johnson County
Located at the confluence of Dry Creek and Powder River, this supply post was in use from 1876 to 1878, serving troops involved in
the Powder River Expedition's winter campaign of 1876–1877,
including those involved in the Dull Knife Battle. The cantonment
had at least forty log structures. This post, established by Captain
Edwin Pollock, Ninth U. S. Infantry, on August 30, 1877, became
Fort McKinney (*see entry*). A community of around one hundred
residents that grew up across the Powder River from the military
post became known as Powder River Crossing.

Canyon Springs Stage Station 🚏 🚃
Weston County
This station on the Cheyenne–Black Hills (Deadwood) stage route
was located near Four Corners off U. S. 385.

Carbon 🚂 ⛺
Carbon County
Located northeast of Elk Mountain, Carbon was the first coal mine
town established on the Union Pacific Railroad in Wyoming. Mines
began operating in 1868 shortly after rail tracks were laid through the
area. Plains Indians—primarily Lakota and Cheyenne—sometimes
threatened the community. In one incident the stable boss was outside town searching for strayed mules when Indians attacked. Other
men from Carbon helped him to safety and alerted miners who:

> . . . ran from door to door gathering the grim-faced women
> and their frightened children. Soon all living in the camp
> were inside or at the mine, the women and children hud-
> dled inside, while the men, above ground, tramped back
> and forth with their hunting rifles swung over their arms
> (*History of the Union Pacific Coal Mines* 1940, np).

Carbon's coal mines remained in operation and the town was
vibrant until the 1890s when a series of fires swept through the town.
Water supplies were limited, and a cholera epidemic killed many

Ruins of a sandstone building remain at the site of Carbon, the first coal mining town along the Union Pacific line in Wyoming. (*Candy Moulton*)

residents, particularly children. The town rebuilt after the fires, but it dwindled after 1902 when the UP laid a new line farther north. Soon Carbon was a ghost of its former self, and some of the frame buildings were relocated to its successor, Hanna. Most of the sandstone slab buildings were simply deserted; some of their walls still remain.

Carter Wagon Road
Uinta County
This wagon road linked Carter with Fort Bridger and generally followed the route of Wyoming Highway 112.

Cattle Kate & James Averill Lynch Site
Natrona and Carbon Counties
James Averill (sometimes spelled Averell) came to Wyoming Territory in the 1860s as a member of Company H, Thirteenth Infantry,

U. S. Army, serving at Fort Fred Steele until he was mustered out. Then Averill re-enlisted, serving in Company D, Ninth Infantry, under General George Crook. He assisted in construction of Fort Reno and Fort McKinney. Later he killed a man in the Buffalo area, and he served jail time before being released and taking up his homestead in the Sweetwater River Valley.

Ellen Watson lived for a time in Denver City and then in Cheyenne before moving to Rawlins, Wyoming, where she cooked and cleaned at the Rawlins House. She moved to the Sweetwater Valley in 1886 where she took up a homestead of her own and, according to some sources, secretly married James Averill (Van Pelt 2003; see also Hufsmith 1993).

Wyoming cattlemen, irritated with both the encroachment of homesteaders on range they considered their own and increased cattle rustling, responded with violence in various areas of Wyoming during the 1880s and 1890s. The claims filed along the Sweetwater River by homesteaders Watson and Averill angered the big cattle ranchers who also had stock in that area. Further, Averill was outspoken in his criticism of the cattlemen, and he wrote to newspapers in the region urging homesteaders to band together to hold their land. The cattlemen claimed that Watson's and Averill's cattle herds seemed to grow more quickly than they should. Finally on a hot afternoon, July 22, 1889, the cattlemen drove a wagon to the homesteaders' property, forced Averill and Watson to climb in, and took the two to a tree where they were hanged.

Although murder charges were brought against six prominent cattlemen—John Durbin, Robert M. Galbraith, Bob Conner, M. Ernest McLean, Tom Sun, and Albert J. Bothwell—the men never went to trial after witnesses either died mysteriously or disappeared.

For many years Watson was portrayed as a prostitute, although there is no evidence to substantiate such a claim.

Central Star Station
Goshen County
This was another name for the Pony Express relay station better known as Nine Mile Station. (*See* Nine Mile Station.)

The Cherokee Trail Wagon Train crosses Carbon County in 2002, following the south branch of the Cherokee Trail west of Saratoga. (*Candy Moulton*)

Cherokee Trail 🚏 ⛺ 🛻
Albany, Carbon, Sweetwater, and Uinta Counties
Gold discoveries in California in January 1848 soon led a flood of travelers to the region. Among those who struck out overland for California were Cherokee Indians from Arkansas and Oklahoma. Although some travelers sought gold, others recognized the trade opportunity in California and took goods and cattle herds over the trail for sale in the rapidly expanding region. They traveled along the basic route of the Santa Fe Trail to Bent's Fort in present Colorado before turning north, crossing Colorado and entering present Wyoming at Virginia Dale south of Laramie. The 1849 trail then continued across the Laramie Plains, swinging around north of the Medicine Bow Mountains and the prominent landmark known as Medicine

The Cherokee Trail is still visible in Carbon County in southern Wyoming. (*Candy Moulton*)

Mountain, now called Elk Mountain. The trail continued generally west on a route roughly parallel to present Interstate 80, passing near or through such communities as Laramie, McFadden, Arlington, Elk Mountain, Rawlins, Rock Springs, and Green River. At Fort Bridger, the trail merged with the California Trail.

A southern branch of the Cherokee Trail, forged in 1850, took a course that was closer to the Wyoming–Colorado border. North of Virginia Dale, it swung around what became Woods Landing and up Woods Creek (along Wyoming Route 230) then dropped into North Park, Colorado, before following the east flank of the Sierra Madre Range (again along Wyoming Route 230) passing just north of present Encampment and Riverside then continuing west to Twin Groves (west of present Saratoga) before turning south again. The trail was north of present Baggs and wove its way west to the Green River and eventually Fort Bridger.

The 1850 route was sometimes close to the 1849 route in western Wyoming, but at times it was many miles to the south. Other routes also are part of the Cherokee Trail system as it crosses Wyoming, some of them in use for only a single year or a single crossing by travelers. In later years, the Overland Trail followed portions of the Cherokee Trail across Wyoming. (*See* Overland Trail.)

Cheyenne–Black Hills (Deadwood) Stage Route 🚂 🚃
Laramie, Platte, Goshen, Niobrara, Weston, and Crook Counties
Following discovery of gold in the Black Hills in 1874, miners began pushing into the region even though it was technically off-limits since it was a part of the Great Sioux Reservation under terms of the 1868 Treaty at Fort Laramie. Soon after the rush to the Hills started, communities began vying for position as jump-off points. Cheyenne, in southern Wyoming Territory, quickly took a leading role because it had access to the Union Pacific Railroad that passed through town. As a result, a freighter road or route quickly became established, linking Cheyenne with Deadwood in Dakota Territory (now South Dakota). Stage service ran each Monday and Thursday. Passengers loaded and unloaded in front of the InterOcean Hotel in downtown Cheyenne, just a block from the Union Pacific Railroad Terminal. One reason so much freight and so many passengers took the Cheyenne–Deadwood route, rather than routes from Nebraska communities, was the construction of an iron military bridge over the North Platte River near Fort Laramie in 1875. That bridge made it easier for travelers to cross the river; therefore, they chose the Cheyenne to Deadwood route instead of the trail from Sidney in western Nebraska.

The Cheyenne–Deadwood route passed through or near Cheyenne, Fort Laramie, Lusk, and Mule Creek Junction. Among the stations on the route were Chug Water Ranch, Running Water, Rawhide Buttes, Silver Cliff, and Hat Creek. The route left Cheyenne and traveled north past such landmarks and stage stations as Horse Creek, Bear Springs, Chugwater, Chug Springs, Eagle's Nest, Fort Laramie, Rawhide Buttes, Hat Creek, Robber's Roost, Cheyenne Crossing, and Jenney Stockade before entering

Dakota Territory and continuing through Custer City to Deadwood (Spring 1948).

Chug Water Ranch 🚃
Platte County

John "Portugee" Phillips, a descendent of Portuguese parents who was born on Pico, an island in the Azores, opened Chug Water Ranch as a station on the Cheyenne to Deadwood stage route in March 1876. Phillips had other business interests in the area, operating the Chug Water Hotel and serving as postmaster. Earlier he had engaged in some Wyoming mining exploration and made a ride for assistance for the troops at Fort Phil Kearny in 1866 after the battle involving Lieutenant William J. Fetterman. For a time Phillips also freighted military goods in the Fort Laramie area. In 1878, he sold his business interests to Hambleton & Company of Baltimore, Maryland, for $16,000. He then relocated to Cheyenne, where he died on November 18, 1883. (*See also* Portugee Phillips' Ride.)

Church Buttes 🚃
Sweetwater County

This landmark on the Oregon–Mormon Trail was the site of a Pony Express relay station in 1860 and 1861. It is located about thirty miles west of Green River.

Cold Springs Station 🚃
Goshen County

Located about two miles southeast of Torrington, this was an Overland Stage relay station from 1859 through 1862 and also served as a Pony Express relay stop in 1860 and 1861. It also went by the names Spring Ranch Station, Torrington Station, and Junction House. A trading post operated by John Jamason was about a half mile east of the station (Goering 1970).

Connor Battlefield, 1865 ⚔ 🏴 Λ
Sheridan County

The site of the Connor Battlefield is now a state park in the community of Ranchester. On August 28, 1865, Arapahos under the leadership of Old David and Black Bear were encamped at the site when army troops led by Major General P. E. Connor attacked without provocation. The subsequent battle led to destruction of around 250 Arapaho lodges plus the deaths of many Arapahos, including women and children. This is also called the Battle of Tongue River.

Cooper Creek Station 🛒
Albany County
Dwight Fisk managed this Overland Trail station located about twenty-five miles east of Fort Halleck on today's Albany–Carbon county line near the present Cooper Cove Rest Area beside Interstate 80. Fisk's wife lived at the station as well, giving birth to a premature baby girl on August 30, 1864. Delivered by the Fort Halleck Post Surgeon, Dr. J. H. Finfrock, the baby lived only a couple of hours. In another tragic incident, Mrs. Fisk witnessed the murder of Fort Halleck cook Hod Russell by Bob Jennings, a man described as an outlaw and also a "Galvanized Yankee," that is, a former Confederate prisoner who was released so long as he joined the frontier army to serve in the West. Jennings was apparently not in the army at the time of the killing. He was taken into custody by frontiersman Bill Comstock. Though she was subpoenaed to testify at the trial, Mrs. Fisk was not required to do so. At trial Jennings pled guilty. He was subsequently hanged, though whether that was accomplished as a judgment for his guity plea or whether he was lynched by a mob from Cooper Creek Station is unclear (Jones 2005).

Cottonwood Station 🛒
Platte County
This Pony Express relay station located on private land northwest of present Guernsey is sometimes called Bitter Cottonwood Stage Station (Carley 1953).

Crazy Woman, Battle of ⚓ ▆ ⛺
Johnson County
Approximately 150 Lakota warriors attacked a wagon train and a military escort led by Lieutenant George Templeton in this battle July 20, 1866, near Crazy Woman Creek south of Buffalo. In the

fighting, Indians killed Lieutenant Napoleon H. Daniels and Sergeant Ferrell and injured many other soldiers and members of the wagon train. As the attack started, the wagon train circled and the men dug rifle pits for protection. The wagon train had twenty-nine men, three women, and one child. The attack was broken off when two companies of troops arrived from Fort Reno.

Crook Campaign, 1876 ⊤ ▀ ⩕
Sheridan County

General George Crook set up a camp in May 1876 at the confluence of Little Goose and Big Goose Creeks in present Sheridan as he traveled north as part of a three-prong wave of soldiers intent on locating hostile Indians believed to be camped farther north. Crook's command, which was a part of the Powder River Expedition, left the Goose Creek campsite on July 17, pushing north into Montana Territory where they engaged in the Battle of the Rosebud, losing decisively to Lakota and Cheyenne warriors. Subsequently, Crook retreated to a new camp on the east flank of Wyoming's Big Horn Mountains. As a result he did not take part in the ill-fated battle of the Greasy Grass, also known as the Battle of the Little Bighorn, on June 25, when Lakota and Cheyenne warriors united against the Seventh Cavalry Command of Lieutenant Colonel George Armstrong Custer, killing Custer's entire command.

Crook subsequently ranged through northeast Wyoming seeking hostile tribesmen before traveling east into Dakota Territory. There his troops were involved in the Battle of Slim Buttes, where they overtook a Lakota camp, engaging in the first military-Indian fight after the battle at the Little Bighorn. After Slim Buttes, the Crook command continued south to Deadwood, struggled through muddy conditions caused by heavy rains, ran out of food, and killed their horses to provide sustenance. Their struggles as they approached Deadwood became known as the Mud March, Starvation March, and Horsemeat March. Crook left the command before reaching Deadwood, but his command remained intact and ultimately traveled through the Black Hills to Fort Robinson in western Nebraska.

Crooks Gap 🌲
Fremont County

This break in the Green Mountains, located west of Jeffrey City, is named for General George Crook, who served in Wyoming during the Powder River Expedition of 1876.

Crowheart Butte ☨ 𝕬 🌲
Fremont County

Located east of Crowheart and north of U. S. 26/287, the distinctive Crowheart Butte received its name in Crow and Shoshone legend for a battle in 1857 between Crow Chief Big Robber and Shoshone Chief Washakie. The fight ended when Washakie killed Big Robber and then reportedly ate the Crow's heart, although the Shoshones, including members of Washakie's family, say he did not eat the heart but instead returned to camp with it on his lance.

Custer Expedition, 1874 ☨ 🏴 ⌁
Crook County

In 1874, on a reconnaissance of the Black Hills of present South Dakota and Wyoming to determine resources in the region, Lieutenant Colonel George Armstrong Custer and his men traveled the region that now includes Newcastle, Sundance, and Hulett. While camped on Inyan Kara Creek July 22 and 23, Custer climbed Inyan Kara Mountain and carved his name there. Two soldiers died and were buried nearby before Custer proceeded north to Spring Creek—a site he named Floral Valley because of the profusion of wild flowers.

Deep Rut Hill 🚃
Platte County

(*See* Oregon Trail Ruts.)

Deer Creek Station ☨ 🚃
Converse County

Deer Creek was a popular and good camping spot on the Oregon–California–Mormon Trail. On July 16, 1849, J. Goldsborough Bruff, who was headed to the California gold fields, was at Deer Creek along with hundreds of other people who were also rushing to find their fortune. He describes the scene:

> [W]e crossed, passing through hundreds of tents, wagons, camp fires, and people of every age & sex, congregated on its banks, and turned down to the right, camped on the banks of the Platte, at the Ferry. . . . (Bruff 1849, as quoted in Haines 1981, 176).

Bruff also writes that the amount of property and supplies travelers abandoned at Deer Creek to lighten their loads and travel more quickly to their destinations was "extraordinary."

In 1857 Joseph Bisonette built Deer Creek Station, which had a store, post office, and blacksmith shop. Bisonette also operated a ferry service across the North Platte River at a location just north and slightly west of the station.

John M. Hockaday and Company obtained a U. S. mail contract in 1858, subsequently establishing a route along the Oregon–California road and thirty-six stations to serve the mail delivery operation. One of those stations was Deer Creek Station, begun not far from the location of the Upper Platte River Indian Agency that was operated by Indian Agent Thomas Twiss.

Reaching the area in August 1860, Sir Richard F. Burton writes:

> The station boasts of an Indian agent, Major Twiss, a post-office, a store, and of course a grog-shop. M. Bissonette, the owner of the two latter and an old Indian trader, was the usual Creole, speaking a French not unlike that of the Channel Islands, and wide awake to the advantages derivable from travelers. . . . I wish my enemy no more terrible fate than to drink excessively with M. Bissonette of M. Bissonette's liquor (Burton 1862; reprint 1990, 138–139).

The station served stagecoach traffic and was a Pony Express station in 1860 and 1861. In 1866, Lakota Indians killed three men and burned the Deer Creek Station, according to a reference to the incident by artist William Henry Jackson, who traveled through the area that year (Jackson 1940).

Devil's Gate 🌱 🌲 🚃
Natrona County

The Sweetwater River flows through this rock canyon that was a landmark to overland trail travelers in the mid-1800s. Access to the area is open to the public through the Handcart Ranch operated by the Church of Jesus Christ of Latter-day Saints. Devil's Gate is about 60 miles north of Rawlins and 60 miles southwest of Casper near Wyoming Highway 220.

Devil's Gate Fort 🚃
Natrona County

(*See* Seminoe's Fort.)

Devil's Gate Station 🚃
Natrona County

Known as U. S. Mail Station No. 29, Devil's Gate Station also served stagecoach travelers on the overland trails in the 1850s and 1860s. It was a relay station for the Pony Express in 1860 and 1861.

Devils Tower 🌱 🌲
Crook County

The volcanic cone that is Devils Tower is a site considered sacred by Lakota, Cheyenne, Kiowa, Arapaho, and Crow Indians. For the Kiowas it is Tso-aa "Tree Rock," to the Crows it is Dabicha "Bear's Lair," to the Arapahos and Cheyennes it is Bear's Tipi. The Lakota call it Mato Tipila "Bear's Lodge." The first ascent by people of European descent occurred July 4, 1893, when William "Bill" Rogers and W. A. Ripley scaled the columns that make up the tower by using an oak peg ladder. Subsequently they placed a flag on top. Rogers' wife, Linnie, was the first woman known to climb the tower, making her way to the top on July 4, 1895. A U. S. Geological Survey party visiting the site in 1875 under command of Colonel Richard I. Dodge gave it the modern name.

Wyoming Senator Francis E. Warren expressed concern about protecting the geological site when he wrote the Commissioner of the General Land office in February 1892, asking for protection of both Devils Tower and the Little Missouri Buttes. A subsequent Forest Reserve Act established slightly more than sixty acres, including both landmarks, as a temporary forest reserve. Senator Warren in July took another step in the preservation process when he introduced a bill to establish "Devils Tower National Park"; however, the bill was not approved. In 1906 the issue was revived after passage of the Antiquities Act when U. S. Representative Frank W. Mondell, chairman of the House Committee on Public Lands, threw his support behind the proposal. On September 24, 1906, President Theodore Roosevelt proclaimed Devils Tower a national monument—the first in the nation. Little Missouri Buttes was not included in the proclamation, and the remainder of the forest reserve was opened for settlement in 1908 (Mattison 1955, 54).

Devils Tower is twelve miles southwest of Hulett off Wyoming Highway 24.

Dillon
Carbon County

Miners working at the Rudefeha mine in the Grand Encampment Copper District moved a mile down Haggarty Creek and started a new town when the copper company officials decided to prohibit the sale of alcohol in Rudefeha. The new town soon had a boarding house, and because owner Malachi Dillon threw in free meals for people who stayed and drank at his establishment, the town quickly took his name. Now a ghost town with just a few crumbling log walls and indentations in the earth representing structure foundations, Dillon is in the Medicine Bow–Routt National Forest and can be reached by taking Wyoming Highway 70 west from Encampment, or east from Savery, to Forest Road 862, just west of Haggarty Creek, and then following that road 2.5 miles to the north.

Downington 🚙
Carbon County

Located about ten miles southeast of Encampment, this community served as a stop on the stage and freight line between Grand Encampment and Big Creek. It had a store, hotel, and post office as well as other structures all near the banks of Beaver Creek just off the

The Dug Springs Station, like most stations on the Oregon Trail, had walls made with stones found nearby. (*Candy Moulton*)

Cherokee Trail. Lieutenant John C. Frémont and his men camped near here in 1844. Today one can see only foundations of the buildings as indentations in the ground. The site is on private ranch land.

Dry Sandy Station
Sweetwater County
This was a Pony Express relay station in 1860 and 1861. (*See* Pony Express Trail.)

Duck Lake Station
Carbon County
This station served the Overland Trail. (*See* Overland Trail.)

Dug Springs Station
Sweetwater County
This Overland Trail station also went by the name Barrel Springs Station. Some emigrants also called it Puffin' Bull, for the way oxen

breathed after pulling heavy wagons up the hill toward the station when they were headed west. Built of sandstone rocks, this station also had a rock corral. Located in Middle Barrel Springs Canyon, the area had numerous wild rose bushes, so it was also sometimes known as Wild Rose Station (Winter 1961). (*See* Overland Trail.)

Dull Knife Battle 🍴 🏳 Ⱥ
Johnson County

Cheyenne Chief Dull Knife and Arapaho Chief Little Wolf camped with their followers south of Fraker Mountain, west of present Kaycee and midway between Barnum and Mayoworth, in the fall of 1876. There on the cold, wintry night of November 25, Colonel Ranald Mackenzie and Fourth Cavalry troops that included Pawnee, Shoshone, Cheyenne, and Lakota scouts, attacked the camp. Mackenzie was following the orders of Brigadier General George Crook, Commander of the U. S. Army's Department of the Platte, who had determined that the way to subdue hostile Indians was to strike them in their winter camps, destroying their lodges and supplies, including food, before stealing horses. Crook believed that without means of shelter and support, the Indians would be forced to move onto reservations.

The Cheyenne warriors, and even some Cheyenne women, fought valiantly before fleeing their ravaged camp, striking out through the cold and snowy weather and traveling through Fraker Pass to make their way the seventy miles north where they found refuge with Crazy Horse's non-reservation band of Lakotas.

Captain John G. Bourke, with Mackenzie's command, writes in *On the Border with Crook*:

> In the gray twilight of a cold November morning (the 25th), Mackenzie with the cavalry and Indian scouts burst like a tornado upon the unsuspecting village of the Cheyennes . . . and wiped it from the face of the earth. There were two hundred and five lodges, each of which was a magazine of supplies of all kinds—buffalo and pony meat, valuable robes, ammunition, saddles, and the comforts of civilization—in appreciable quantities. The roar of the flames exasperated

The Dull Knife Battle took place at this site, which is now private ranch land. (*Courtesy Wyoming State Historic Preservation Office*)

the fugitive Cheyennes to a frenzy; they saw their homes disappearing in fire and smoke. . . .

Seven hundred and five ponies fell into our hands and were driven off the field; as many more were killed and wounded or slaughtered by the Cheyennes the night after the battle, partly for food and partly to let their half-naked old men and women put their feet and legs in the warm entrails.

We lost one officer, Lieutenant John A. McKinney, Fourth Cavalry, and six men killed and twenty-five men wounded; the enemy's loss was unknown (1891; reprint 1971, 392–393).

The Cheyennes eventually surrendered and reported that around forty people had died in Mackenzie's attack on their camp. The site of the battle is on private land southwest of Mayoworth.

Elk Horn Station
Platte County

This was a relay station for the Pony Express. (*See* Pony Express Trail.)

Elk Mountain, Cheyenne Attack on Fletcher Family, 1865
Carbon County

The Fletcher family ran into trouble while following the Overland Trail between Arlington and Elk Mountain in 1865. Cheyenne Indians attacked the train of about seventy-five wagons the Fletchers were traveling with. In the initial attack, Mrs. Fletcher was killed, her husband was wounded, and the Indians took daughters Amanda Mary, thirteen, and Lizzie, two, as captives. After the incident, the wagon train continued on to Salt Lake City. A year later a white trader won Amanda Fletcher's release when he reportedly paid $1,600 and gave the Indians a gun and a horse. She rejoined her father in Salt Lake City. Lizzie had been separated from her sister soon after the attack. Some thirty-five years later, the two sisters were reunited, although Lizzie, who was married to an Arapaho man (and did not remember her sister), refused to leave him to go with Amanda.

Elk Mountain, Wyoming Lawmen Killed by Outlaws, 1878
Carbon County

The first two Wyoming peace officers killed in the line of duty met their demise in an aspen grove on the west side of Elk Mountain in August 1878. "Big Nose" George Parrott, "Dutch Charley" Burris, and some accomplices attempted to derail a Union Pacific train east of Carbon, then they fled toward Elk Mountain when a section boss detected their scheme and notified the Carbon County sheriff.

Deputies Tip Vincent and Robert Widdowfield set out on the trail of the would-be robbers along with a larger posse. After some effort at trailing the gang, the posse disbanded, leaving only Vincent and Widdowfield to continue the pursuit. The two Carbon County deputies caught up with the would-be bandits, who had established a camp in the trees on the west side of Elk Mountain. When the deputies rode up to the foothills camp, they were ambushed and killed. The robbers immediately fled the scene, riding north toward

Hole-in-the-Wall country, a refuge for outlaws for many years because of its isolation and limited access.

When Vincent and Widdowfield failed to return to Rawlins, a search party headed to Elk Mountain. They found the bodies of the lawmen in an area that is now private ranchland and returned them to Rawlins for burial. Subsequently, efforts began to find their killers. Authorities arrested "Dutch Charley" in Montana two years later, and Carbon County Sheriff James G. Rankin went to bring him back to Carbon County to face justice. At Carbon, vigilantes stopped the train Rankin and "Dutch Charley" were riding, taking the outlaw off the train and hanging him from a telegraph pole. Miner John Milliken was present at the hanging and writes:

> They left him hanging there until the next day. The wind was blowing hard all night, and the body swung back and forth, back and forth all night, hitting the [telegraph] pole each time with such force that by morning the face was horrible mashed (as quoted in Moulton 1995, 245).

Later U. S. Marshal John X. Beidler arrested "Big Nose" George Parrott in Miles City, Montana, and Carbon County deputies went there to return him to Wyoming to face trial for the murders of Vincent and Widdowfield. At Carbon, vigilantes again stopped the train and prepared for a lynching. Parrott, unlike Burris, confessed that he and his cohorts had planned to rob the train and later had killed the deputies. The mob did not lynch Parrott, and he was returned to Rawlins August 7, 1880. On September 13, he pleaded guilty to killing the lawmen, but he recanted four days later. Then on November 18, he again said he was guilty. Accepting that declaration, on December 15 the judge sentenced Parrott to hang on April 2, 1881.

The outlaw did not live that long. On March 22, 1881, he attempted to escape from the Carbon County jail by attacking Sheriff Rankin. The sheriff's wife, Rosa, heard her husband call out about the escape attempt and slammed the heavy cell door shut. The incident was too much for the citizens of Rawlins. They gathered outside the jail and between 10 and 11 P.M., knocked on the door indicating that "friends" wanted to visit. When the guard refused entry, the mob forced its way through the door. The vigilantes took

Parrott with them from the jail and headed to Front Street where they stopped at a telegraph pole near the J. W. Hugus Store. There they quickly threw a rope over the pole, tied it around Parrott's neck, and placed him atop a barrel, which they kicked from beneath him when the rope was ready. However, Parrott fell to the ground unharmed in part because the rope had been too long so his feet touched the ground when the barrel was removed. The mob then had to obtain a ladder, reattach the rope, and try a second time. This time the lynching was successful.

After the death of "Big Nose" George Parrott, two local doctors, Union Pacific surgeon Dr. John Osborne and Union Pacific surgeon-physician Dr. Thomas G. Mahgee, accompanied by fifteen-year-old Lillian Heath, who was studying medicine under Dr. Mahgee, took the body. They conducted an autopsy and subsequently skinned the body, making a pair of shoes from some of Parrott's hide and turning his skullcap into an ashtray, pipe, or key holder. Mahgee's motivation for the autopsy, which included cutting the skull and removing the brain, was to study the brain of a criminal in an effort to cure his wife who had been kicked in the head by a horse and sustained brain damage that left her with a diagnosis of criminal insanity, according to Carbon County Historian Rans Baker.[2] Later most of Parrott's bones were placed in a whiskey barrel and buried in Rawlins, where they were unearthed decades later. Meanwhile, the shoes were worn by Osborne when he was inaugurated as Wyoming governor, and eventually they became a museum curiosity and remain in the collection of the Carbon County Museum in Rawlins.

Elk Mountain Station
Carbon County

This was a station on the Overland Trail near the present town of Elk Mountain. (*See* Overland Trail.)

Embar
Hot Springs County

This 1885-era post office was established on the ranch of Colonel Robert A. Torrey, who organized Torrey's Rough Riders for service in the Spanish-American War. The ranch brand was an M⁻, so the ranch and post office went by the name Embar. The ranch, north-west of Thermopolis, is still in operation.

Evans Pass Fight with Indians, 1865 🅐 🚂
Albany and Laramie Counties

Union Pacific Railroad surveyors fought with Indians in this area west of present Cheyenne in 1865. As they retreated, the surveyors passed a lone pine tree growing from a rock, which led them to a natural pass that became the route of the transcontinental railroad. General Grenville M. Dodge subsequently named the pass for sur-veyor and civil engineer James A. Evans.

Evanston 🚂
Uinta County

Evanston started as a Union Pacific hell-on-wheels town when Harvey Booth pitched a tent November 23, 1868, and opened a restaurant, hotel, and saloon to serve the six hundred or so "camp fol-lowers" who moved west with the railroad construction. The town prospered as a line division camp on the Union Pacific. It boasted a large Chinese population.

Expedition Island 🛶
Sweetwater County

Located in present Green River, this island served as the beginning point for John Wesley Powell's 1869 exploratory journey down the Green River. In specially built boats christened the *No Name*, *Kitty Clyde's Sister*, *Maid of the Cañon*, and, the pilot craft, *Emma Dean*, Powell and his nine-man crew left Expedition Island on May 24, 1869. That first journey was only partly successful as the party encountered difficulties when the *No Name* wrecked on June 8 and many supplies were lost. Along the trip, some members of the party left the water route and continued overland only to be ambushed and killed by Indians. Those who stayed on the river completed their journey at the confluence of the Virgin and Colorado Rivers.

Subsequently, Powell received authorization—and funding—for a second exploratory trip down the Green River, which he undertook in 1871 and again started from this area near Green River. Expedition Island is a National Historic Place and a Green River City Park, accessible via a walking path and a bridge over the river.

Fetterman Fight 🕇 🏴 Å
Johnson County

On December 21, 1866, Sioux warriors led by Red Cloud lured a military command under Lieutenant William J. Fetterman away from Fort Phil Kearny and over Lodge Trail Ridge. Once the troops were out of sight of the fort, the Indians surrounded the troops, who made a final stand on a hillside located adjacent to U. S. 87 about fifteen miles north of present Buffalo.

Fetterman had orders not to cross over Lodge Trail Ridge, but as he reached the hogback north of the fort, several Indians, possibly including Crazy Horse, rode out. Acting as decoys, they lured the troops over the hill and into a cleverly designed trap. The troops were soon surrounded by a superior force that had planned the attack carefully so as to have the advantage. Troops back at the fort could hear the firing, and a relief/rescue command led by Captain Tenodore Ten Eyck was launched immediately. But by the time those soldiers reached the hillside where Fetterman's command had been surrounded, they found all of the soldiers dead, most from Indian bullets and arrows. But some had apparently taken their own lives rather than be captured or tortured by the Indians.

Though the incident has long since been called the Fetterman Massacre, it really was a fight or battle between enemy forces with the Indians winning a decided victory. When Ten Eyck returned to Fort Phil Kearny with the news of Fetterman's defeat, Colonel Henry Carrington prepared to defend the fort by giving weapons to cooks, orderlies, and even the men who had been held in the fort's guard house. The colonel then made plans to get word of the disaster to other authorities. Subsequently John "Portugee" Phillips and Daniel Dixon, two civilians who had come to the area on a mining venture, rode for help. Dixon had been working as a mail carrier and post guide earning $10 per day. Before the ride for help that placed him permanently in the annals of Wyoming history, Phillips had been a civilian with no government service.

There was a full moon when the two men left Fort Phil Kearny and rode first to Fort Reno then to Horseshoe Station. Other men, including Robert Bailey, accompanied them between Fort Reno and Horseshoe Station. News of the Fetterman fight had been telegraphed ahead from Horseshoe Station, but while at Fort Reno, Lieutenant Colonel Henry Wessels had given Phillips additional dispatches to carry to Fort Laramie. So after a rest at Horseshoe Station, he went on alone the final forty miles to arrive at Fort Laramie on Christmas Eve (Monnett 2008). According to records of Fort Commander Henry Carrington, Phillips and Dixon were paid $300 each for making the journey of approximately 235 miles (*see also* Portugee Phillips' Ride).

In response to the news of the battle, Lieutenant Colonel Henry Wessels was ordered from Fort Reno to Fort Phil Kearny along with two companies of cavalry and four companies of infantry. In the aftermath, Colonel Carrington was relieved of duty at Fort Phil Kearny.

The site of the Fetterman fight is now marked with a large rock monolith beside U.S. 87 north of Buffalo and Fort Phil Kearny.

First White Man's Cabin
Natrona County

When Robert Stuart and six companions headed east from Astoria, Oregon, toward St. Louis in 1812, they crossed what is now central Wyoming. As the travelers struck the river that later became the North Platte, they decided to build a cabin in which they could spend the winter. At a site thought to be near Bessemer Bend about six miles west of Casper, they constructed their shelter. But when a party of Indians, believed to be Arapahos, came to the intended winter campsite, Stuart and his companions, wanting to avoid any potential conflict, left their cabin and continued traveling east, eventually wintering at a site near the present Wyoming–Nebraska border east of Torrington.

Fort Antonio
Johnson County

This is one of several names for a trading site on the upper Powder River operated by Antonio Matéo. Matéo was a trader with

Captain Benjamin L. E. Bonneville but remained in the region after Bonneville departed. (*See also* Portuguese Houses.)

Fort Augur 🌾 🏴
Fremont County

A forerunner to Camp Brown, Fort Augur (also called Camp Augur) is named for General Christopher C. Augur. (*See also* Fort Brown.)

Fort Bernard 🛶
Goshen County

Joseph Bisonette built this trading post in the summer of 1845 to compete with Fort John, operated by the American Fur Company. As was the case during the fur trade era, posts were often referred to as forts, although they were not affiliated with the military. John Baptiste Richard ran the post, which burned during the winter of 1847, though there may have been some later use at the site. Historian and writer Francis Parkman visited the site in 1846, describing it as a "rough structure of logs" built to form a hollow square with rooms for storage and lodging (Paden 1943, 154). Writing in 1850, E. A. Thompkins describes the site as an "assemblage of log huts surrounded by great piles of buffalo hides, the size and shape of eastern haystacks" (Paden 1943, 155). Fort Bernard was located about five miles southeast of Fort Laramie.

Fort Bonneville 🌾 🛶 🛒
Sublette County

In 1832 Captain Benjamin L. E. Bonneville, a baldheaded thirty-seven-year-old French-born West Point graduate, established this fort above the confluence of Horse Creek and the Green River. Bonneville took a two-year leave from the U. S. Army to explore in the West and determine American fur trade potential in the Rocky Mountain region. The official stated mission was to identify streams, locate Indian tribes, and visit both American and British outposts to determine how to open the country to the American fur trade.

Bonneville began his explorations in Independence, Missouri, on May 1, 1832, traveling the route of what would become the Oregon Trail toward Pierre's Hole in present Idaho. Accompanying him were

110 men and several wagons, which are believed to be the first wagons to cross South Pass, the region in central Wyoming that became the main passage for emigrants to Oregon, Utah, and California. On the Green River in July 1832, Bonneville saw buffalo carcasses throughout the area. Although he did go on to Pierre's Hole, Bonneville first established the fort that took his name overlooking the Green River Valley. Strategically it was a good location, and in July it was a pleasant place to be, but Bonneville did not realize the kind of winter weather common to that area. Located in a valley, the cold air of the region combined with winds and snowstorms that swept the region beginning in October and continuing through March. After the first winter, Bonneville realized his strategic location was in a harsh climate; Fort Bonneville became known as Fort Nonsense, or Bonneville's Folly.

A description of the fort, which had blockhouses at two corners, comes from W. A. Ferris, a clerk with the Rocky Mountain Fur Company:

> [The fort had] posts or pickets firmly set in the ground, of a foot or more in diameter, planted close to each other, and about fifteen feet [wide]. . . . The whole together seems well calculated for the security both of men and horses (Ferris 1940, np, as quoted in Moulton 1995, 43).

The fort was in use until 1839. Mountain men held six summer rendezvous nearby, and the first Roman Catholic mass celebrated in what is today Wyoming took place nearby as well. The site of Fort Bonneville is just south of the town of Daniel.

Fort Bridger ⎈ 🛒
Uinta County
Jim Bridger and Louis Vasquez began serving overland emigration in 1842 when they built the trading post that became Fort Bridger. As emigrant Joel Palmer notes in his journal on July 25, 1845:

> [E]ncamped near Fort Bridger. . . . It is built of poles and daubed with mud . . . a shabby concern. Here are about 25 lodges of Indians, or rather white trappers' lodges occupied

Artist Merritt Dana Houghton made this drawing of Jim Bridger's original trading post based on descriptions of it, as the original post had been
burned long before Houghton worked in Wyoming in the 1890s. (*Courtesy Wyoming State Museum*)

by their trapper wives. They have a good supply of robes,
dressed deer, elk and antelope skins, coats, pants, pork, powder, lead, blankets, butcher-knives, spirits, hats, ready-made
clothes, coffee, sugar, etc. They ask for a horse from twenty-
five to fifty dollars in trade. . . . At this place the bottoms are
wide, and covered with good grass. Cotton-wood timber in
plenty. The stream abounds with trout (Palmer 1847, as
quoted in Moulton 1995, 287).

Bridger was involved with the operation of Fort Bridger until
1853 when it was taken over by Mormons. Friction had existed
between Brigham Young, President of the Church of Jesus Christ of
Latter-day Saints, and Bridger for some time due to a number of factors, among them Young's belief that Bridger stirred Indians to
attack Mormon settlements and reported on Mormon activities to
United States authorities. Bridger claimed the Mormons stole his
fort, although the Mormons said they bought it. At any rate, the
Mormons did control Fort Bridger from 1853 until the fall of 1857

when U. S. Army troops marched to the area during the so-called Mormon, or Utah, War. At that time, the Mormons withdrew to Utah and Great Salt Lake City, burning the Bridger outpost as well as Fort Supply, another nearby post, so the military would not benefit from the structures when they arrived in the area. After the U. S. military took over Fort Bridger, Jim Bridger was subsequently paid for claims he made regarding the value of the site.

When Colonel Albert Sidney Johnston and the U. S. troops arrived at Fort Bridger's burned ruins, they established Camp Scott a couple of miles to the north. Lacking supplies, Johnston ordered Captain Randolph B. Marcy to take troops and march to Fort Union in present New Mexico. Marcy's winter journey through Colorado was harrowing as the troops foundered in deep snow and suffered in cold temperatures. Although all their mules died, the party made it to Fort Massachusetts in south-central Colorado where Marcy and his men received aid before they continued on to Fort Union. One man with Marcy died in the effort. Once at Fort Union, Marcy got supplies and returned to Fort Bridger by heading north and striking the route that had been forged by Cherokee Indians in 1849. He made it back to Camp Scott in May of 1858.

The military rebuilt Fort Bridger at the site of Bridger's original trading post under the direction of Major William Hoffman of the Sixth U. S. Infantry; it became an official U. S. Army post on June 7, 1858. The post, later commanded by Major Edward R. S. Canby, was a supply post for the army in Utah, and it subsequently served to protect travelers and was a station on the Overland Trail. Fort Bridger remained in use until May 23, 1878, when it was abandoned, only to be reestablished in June 1880, after the Meeker Massacre and Ute Uprising in northwest Colorado the previous September. It remained active until November 6, 1890 (Frazier 1972).

Fort Brown 🏴
Fremont County

Camp Augur was renamed Fort Brown in 1870, and a year later it was relocated to a site at the junction of the north and south forks of the Little Wind River. The original structures at the first fort were dismantled in 1871, and the salvageable lumber was used for the later facility, which also had log and adobe buildings. Stone and frame buildings were added later. In both cases the forts were named for Captain Frederick H. Brown, who had been killed during the Fetterman battle in December of 1866. By 1872 the facility had a hospital, storehouse, and telegraph office. In 1878 it was renamed Fort Washakie in recognition of the Shoshone chief whose followers settled nearby. (*See also* Camp Augur and Fort Washakie.)

Fort John Buford 🏴
Albany County

Located at the southern edge of present Laramie, Fort John Buford was built in July 1866, a year before the Union Pacific Railroad pushed across southern Wyoming, spawning a series of rail towns, often called hell-on-wheels towns for their open atmosphere.

Established by Captain Henry R. Mizner on July 10, 1866, Fort John Buford became Fort Sanders in September 1866, named for Brigadier General William P. Sanders, who was killed in defense of Knoxville, Tennessee, during the Civil War. (Homsher 1949; Rosenberg 1989; also see Wyoming Recreation Commission 1988).

Fort or Camp Carrington 🏴
Johnson County
(*See* Fort Phil Kearny.)

Fort Caspar 🚩 🏴
Natrona County

Established in 1862 as Platte Bridge Station, the important military post that guarded the crossing of the Oregon–California–Mormon trails and transcontinental telegraph line over the North Platte River, this post became Fort Caspar after a battle July 26, 1865, during which Lieutenant Caspar Collins and five other troops were killed by raiding Cheyenne and Lakota Indians. Collins was the ranking officer involved in the fight. Among the troops stationed here were the Eleventh Ohio Cavalry and the Eighteenth U. S. Infantry, commanded by Captain Richard L. Morris. The post was abandoned October 18, 1867, to be replaced by Fort Fetterman. (*See also* Platte Bridge Station.)

Officers relax at Fort Fetterman, from left: First Lieutenant Henry Seaton, Lieutenant George O. Webster, Lieutenant Henry E. Robinson, and Captain Gebhard L. Luhns, all of the Fourth Infantry, and Captain William H. Andres, Third Cavalry. (*Courtesy Wyoming State Archives*)

Fort Connor 🚏 🏴
Johnson County
(*See* Fort Reno.)

Fort Fetterman 🚏 🏴
Converse County
Named for Brevet Lieutenant Colonel William J. Fetterman, who died December 21, 1866, in battle with Lakota warriors in north-central Wyoming (*see* Fetterman Fight), Fort Fetterman was established July 19, 1867. Major William McIntyre Dye, Fourth U.S. Infantry, commanded the fort located northwest of present Douglas. Troops stationed at Fort Fetterman when it first came into use included the Fourth U.S. Infantry companies A, C, H, and I.

Dick's Place was a saloon at Fetterman after the location was no longer a military post. Several of the men have their guns drawn in what appears to be horseplay for the camera. (*Courtesy Wyoming State Archives*)

Starting in 1876, Fort Fetterman served as a major supply post for troops fighting Indians in the Powder River country to the north. Writing many years later, Sergeant J. O. Ward, Company C, Fourth U. S. Infantry, describes those who participated in the 1876 Powder River Expedition organized at Fort Fetterman:

> This campaign drew the most wonderful collection of frontiersmen that the country ever saw. Among the noted men who accompanied this expedition was Frank Grouard, the chief of all, "Big Batt, Little Batt" [Baptiste Pourier and Baptiste Garnier], Carl Reshaw, Calif. Joe, Buckskin Jack [Joe], Speed Stagner, the Semenoe [*sic*] Bros., Ben Clarke, Liver Eating Johnson, and hundreds of others, more or less famous, including Calamity Jane and her side kicker [*sic*] Frankie Glass.
>
> This wonderful gathering of soldiers, scouts, packers, teamsters and Indians were the guest of Fort Fetterman for seven days. The greatest obstacle was crossing the Platt[e] that was running bank full.

One flat boat that had only one team, operated by cable
that sometimes broke and the boat carried down the river to
be hauled back by men and mules (Ward 1927, 357–364).

The fort was abandoned in 1882, having outlived its need on the
Plains (Frazier 1972). The military reservation was turned over to
the Interior Department on July 22, 1884, and the area became a
civilian outpost, in use as an end point for a freight route linking the
post and area with the Union Pacific Railroad at Rock Creek Station.
Fort Fetterman is now a Wyoming State Park west of Douglas off
Wyoming Route 93.

Fort Halleck 𝍢 ▆ 🚙
Carbon County

Located at the base of Elk Mountain, Fort Halleck was established
July 20, 1862, to protect the telegraph line, travelers on the Over-
land Trail, and the stage route between Denver City and Great Salt
Lake City. It is named for Major General Henry W. Halleck, then
Army Commander of the Department of the Pacific. The site was
selected and the post built by Company A, Eleventh Ohio Volunteer
Cavalry, commanded by Major John O'Ferrall with assistance from
Company D, also of the Eleventh Ohio.

The first units to garrison the post included Companies A and C,
Eleventh Ohio Cavalry (which had formerly been the Sixth Ohio).
Those units built two sets of company quarters, stables adequate for
one hundred horses, officers' quarters, storehouses for the quartermaster and commissary, a sutler's store, a bake house, and a jail.
Those buildings were constructed of rough pine logs, while a hospital and post headquarters were made of hewn logs with lumber for
doors, and window frames freighted in from Fort Laramie.

For a time Fort Halleck was a stage stop on Ben Holladay's
Overland Stage Company line and was managed by the infamous
Jack Slade. After Slade caused problems in the area and was fired by
Ben Holladay, the division was operated by Lem Flowers and later
by Robert Spotswood (Alcorn 1984). It was a difficult post to man
in the winter because of the heavy snow and high winds that are
common in the area.

Fort Halleck was abandoned July 4, 1866, with the military reservation eventually transferred to the Interior Department on October 11, 1886 (Frazier 1972). The fort was located on the north side of Elk Mountain, about three miles west of the present town of Elk Mountain, and now is on private ranch land.

Fort Halleck–Fort Laramie Road 🏴
Carbon, Albany, Platte, and Goshen Counties
Established in 1862 as a link between these two frontier posts, this road was in use until 1866, when Fort Halleck was abandoned.

Fort Hat Creek 🍴 🚂
Niobrara County
Captain James Egan established this fort on Sage Creek in 1875; it later became Hat Creek Station (*see entry*). At the time he located the original fort/station, Egan believed he was on Hat Creek; later he determined the fort was actually on Sage Creek, but the original name stuck. Captain Egan had served with the Second U.S. Cavalry during the Civil War, where he was wounded at Cold Harbor, Virginia. He later served in the West from 1865 through the late 1870s, stationed at Fort Lyon, Colorado, as well as at Fort Sanders, Fort D.A. Russell, and Fort Laramie, all in Wyoming. The Hat Creek fort/station Egan built burned in 1883 to be replaced by a new two-story structure that still stands thirteen miles north of Lusk off U.S. 85.

Fort John 🚂 🛶
Goshen County
In 1841 the American Fur Company built a trading post near the Laramie River, calling it Fort John. The post had fifteen-foot-high adobe walls that enclosed an area some 123 feet by 168 feet. A mile south of Fort Platte, Fort John was a rival of that earlier post. In 1842, when John C. Frémont was at the site, he called the post "Fort John, or Laramie." It was often confused with the more well-known post that succeeded it. In their overland trail journals, both Samuel Parker in 1835 and Francis Parkman in 1846 refer to the site as Fort Laramie. (*See also* Fort Laramie.)

Fort Phil Kearny 🏛 🏴
Johnson County

Located a dozen miles north of present Buffalo, via Interstate 90 and then U. S. 87, Fort Phil Kearny had a brief life as one of three forts established along the tumultuous Bozeman Trail. The fort was established July 16, 1866, under orders from Major General John Pope, commander of the Department of the Missouri. It is named for Major General Philip Kearny, who died in fighting at Chantilly, Virginia, September 1, 1862. The Mountain District, in which the fort was located, was commanded by Colonel Henry B. Carrington, who oversaw construction of the stockaded post, one of few such structures in Wyoming.

Thick logs formed the post stockade with blockhouses on the east and west corners and notches for rifles and other small arms as well as a banquette, or gunner's platform, three feet off the ground on the inside of each wall. Entrance to the stockade was through gates made of heavy wooden planks and smaller wicket gates. Four log barracks had dirt floors and slab roofs covered with dirt. The storehouses and commissary building were frame construction with one-inch boards and mill slabs used for roofing materials. Carrington and his wife, Frances, lived in a large wood frame building that had brick chimneys and a shingle roof. Commissioned officers and their families lived in log huts. There was also a log hospital, a wood-framed headquarters office and quartermaster's office, plus housing for the band, laundresses, citizen employees, and non-commissioned officers. Other buildings included a saddler's shop, cavalry stable, guardhouse, and powder magazine (Murray 1968, as described in Rosenberg 1989).

Two steam-operated sawmills housed in frame buildings covered with slabs were put into use outside the stockade, and several buildings where civilians lived and worked were located outside the stockade as well. Three blockhouses were constructed in the wood-cutting area to provide protection there. In 1867 a log cabin was built three hundred yards from the stockade for use by the Indian Peace Commission (Murray 1968 in Rosenberg 1989).

Troops from the post were involved in a number of important battles that were a part of the First Sioux War, or Red Cloud's War,

Located on the south side of Bitter Creek in Sweetwater County, Fort LaClede served as a station on the Overland Trail. When fully operating, the fort comprised two buildings used by soldiers, plus a lookout tower. All that remains are some of the sandstone rock walls of the main buildings. (*Candy Moulton*)

waged between 1866 and 1868, including the Wagon Box Fight and the Fetterman Fight (*see individual entries*). The army abandoned Fort Phil Kearny in 1868, and after the troops departed, Lakota Indians burned the post. The property is now owned by the state of Wyoming and managed as a State Historic Site.

Fort LaClede 🏚 🏴
Sweetwater County
This station on the Overland Trail was situated on an open flat on the south side of Bitter Creek, some thirteen miles west of Dug Springs. Built of sandstone, Fort LaClede had two main buildings used for soldier quarters and as a gun and lookout tower. A root cellar, rifle pits, and a corral completed the fort complex. A series of rifle pits were dug in the surrounding landscape. Four companies of the Eleventh Ohio Volunteer Cavalry manned Fort LaClede in 1863, patrolling the area between Sulphur Springs and Green River. A skirmish occurred between Indians and Company B, Eleventh Ohio Cavalry, under command of Lieutenant Wade Thorsen in June 1865 about two miles east of the fort. The soldiers who engaged the Indians initially were later assisted by Company D, Eleventh Ohio

Cavalry, and some civilians who were at Fort LaClede at the time (Tierney 1961).

The Eleventh Kansas Cavalry, commanded by Colonel P. B. Plumb, replaced the Eleventh Ohio Volunteers in 1865.

The remains of old Fort LaClede are on public land in a remote area south of Interstate 80 between Rawlins and Rock Springs. The land surrounding the site is leased to the Rock Springs Grazing Association.

Fort Laramie 〒 ▰ 🚜 ⅄
Goshen County

Without doubt, the most important frontier-era military site in present Wyoming is Fort Laramie, three miles west of the present town of Fort Laramie. Begun as a fur trade outpost in 1834 owned and operated by Robert Campbell and William Sublette, the site became a military post in 1849. The oldest extant building in Wyoming is Old Bedlam, a two-story structure built in 1849 that is now restored as part of the structures at Fort Laramie National Historic Site. Soon after construction of Old Bedlam, fort personnel built an adobe sutler's store, which also remains standing and where on hot summer days, modern visitors can enjoy refreshments such as lemonade or sarsaparilla.

Known early as Fort William, for William Sublette, and then Fort John (for John B. Sarpy, a trader), the post became Fort Laramie when a clerk wrote "Fort Laramie" on correspondence rather than "Fort John on the Laramie." When it was still a privately owned fur trade post in 1846, Heinrich Lienhard noted that the post was a rectangular structure with sixteen- to twenty-foot-high walls of dried brick. The interior had various rooms. Passing by the fort in 1846, historian Francis Parkman writes:

> Found ourselves before the gateway of Fort Laramie, under the impending blockhouse erected above it to guard the entrance. . . . The little fort is built of bricks dried in the sun, and externally is of an oblong form, with bastions of clay, in the form of ordinary blockhouses, at two of the corners (Parkman 1846, 84–85).

The ruins of some military era buildings remain at Fort Laramie. (*Candy Moulton*)

John C. Frémont, who visited the site in 1842, recommended that the U. S. military obtain the strategically located post to protect overland trail travel. As a result, in 1849 the military purchased the fort from the American Fur Company for $4,000, turning it into a military post that remained an active garrison until 1890.

Fort Laramie served as a major supply post for people traveling the overland trail routes, it was the site of important Indian treaties negotiated in 1851 and 1868, and it was on the route of not only the Oregon, Mormon, and California trails but also the subsequent Bozeman Trail and the Cheyenne to Deadwood stage route, the latter established after 1875. Because of its strategic location, it was a launch point for many military and scientific expeditions, including the Raynolds Exploration and the Maynadier Expedition of 1859 and the 1875 Black Hills Expedition of Walter P. Jenney and Henry Newton (*see individual entries*).

The sutler's store, right, at Fort Laramie is one of the oldest buildings in Wyoming. (*Candy Moulton*)

Private ferry service over the North Platte River was established in 1849, and later the army had a barge to transport travelers over the river, which passes adjacent to the fort. The first steel bridge across the North Platte River in present Wyoming was installed by military companies in 1875 from Fort Laramie. The bridge remains in place over the river, just east of the fort grounds, though now it is used only by pedestrians.

Because their treaty annuities were distributed at or near Fort Laramie, after the 1851 treaty an encampment of Indians was almost always near the fort.

The military abandoned Fort Laramie in 1890, and area homesteaders then purchased many of the buildings, moving them from their original locations. In 1937 the state of Wyoming obtained the property, subsequently turning it over to the National Park Service, which maintains it as a National Historic Site.

At Fort Laramie, visitors can not only see original buildings and recreations of the early fur trade posts and military structures, but they can also walk in the traces of the emigrant trails that used the fort as a provisioning point.

Fort Laramie Indian Burial Sites 𝕀̌

Goshen County

Sioux Indians had a burial site not far from Fort Laramie. Among the Indians buried at the site was Ah-ho-appa (Falling Leaf), daughter of Brulé chief Spotted Tail, who died of tuberculosis in the fall of 1866. Fort Laramie's commanding officer, Colonel H. E. Maynadier, gave permission for the burial platform that held Ah-ho-appa. Colonel Maynadier accompanied Chief Spotted Tail to the burial ceremony, and military rites were held for the Indian woman in recognition of her father's stature in the tribe. An important Indian tree burial site was located within view of the fort as well. Some Northern Plains tribes did not inter dead people but instead placed them on scaffolds or on platforms built in trees, as was the case with this burial site. Some sources called this the "papoose tree" due to the number of child burials.

Fort Laramie Indian Peace Conference, 1866 ▤ 𝕀̌

Indian and military representatives gathered at Fort Laramie on June 5, 1866, with a goal of resolving differences between the tribes—particularly the Lakota—and the travelers making their way across the Bozeman Trail that cut through the Powder River Basin. The talks broke down eight days later with the arrival of Colonel Henry B. Carrington and troops he commanded. The Indians considered this a breach of faith as the soldiers meant to occupy forts only then under negotiation in the treaty were already moving forward. Oglala leader Red Cloud refused to meet with Carrington, believing the troops would take the Indian lands under any circumstances. Holding his rifle as he led his warriors away from the conference, Red Cloud is reported to have said, "In this and the Great Spirit I trust for the right" (Doane 1928, 536). Subsequent battles took place between the frontier military and Red Cloud's warriors in the period that became known as Red Cloud's War, a war that would end in a defeat for the United States.

When Carrington led his troops away from Fort Laramie and north toward Powder River country on June 17, 1866, he may not have understood the passion the Lakota and Cheyenne people had for the Powder River Basin. The day previous, Carrington wrote the following to Lieutenant Colonel H. G. Litchfield:

> All the Commissioners agree that I go to occupy a region which the Indians will only surrender for a great equivalent. Even my arrival has started among them many absurd rumors, but I apprehend no serious difficulty. Patience, forebearance, and common sense in dealing with the Sioux and Cheyennes, will do much with all who really desire peace, but it is indispensable that ample supplies of ammunition come promptly (National Archives & Records Administration n.d., 1).

Carrington refused an offer of assistance by Cheyenne warriors, and almost immediately the attacks began. Just one day out on the trail toward Powder River, Carrington's columns and wagon train were attacked by Lakota warriors. The fighting resulted in the deaths of two soldiers, injuries to two others, and the loss of 187 head of livestock. It was the beginning of two years of nearly constant battles. As Grace Raymond Hebard and E. A. Brininstool write in *The Bozeman Trail*, "[T]here never was a day, never an hour, but that the Indians attacked, or would have attacked if not properly watched" (1922a, 271).

Fort Laramie Treaty, 1851 🏳️ ⩜

The first major agreement between Plains Indians and the U. S. government was negotiated near Fort Laramie in 1851. Approximately 10,000 Indians from numerous tribes, including the Sioux, Cheyenne, Crow, Arapaho, Mandan, Arikara, Gros Ventre, and Assiniboine, gathered along the North Platte and Laramie Rivers near Fort Laramie to begin talks about territories and travel across the emigrant trails. The Indians had so many horses that the pastures near Fort Laramie were soon denuded of grass, so the Indians relocated downstream on the North Platte to near Horse Creek along the present Wyoming–Nebraska border just north of U. S. 26. There the actual negotiations finally took place. As a result of the treaty, the Indians agreed that various territories would be established for each of their tribes; they also agreed to allow the roads leading to Oregon,

California, and Utah. Among other provisions, the Indians agreed "to abstain in future from all hostilities whatever against each other, to maintain good faith and friendship in all their mutual intercourse, and to make an effective and lasting peace." In exchange for the treaty concessions, the tribes were to receive annuities of $50,000 per year for fifty years. But the treaty terms were changed by the U. S. Senate before ratification, so the tribes received the annuity payments for only ten years. The Crow tribe did not accept the new treaty terms.

One difficulty in negotiating such treaties, as the U. S. government soon realized, was that even though a particular chief or headman might sign his name or make his mark on a treaty document, he was speaking only for himself and not necessarily for all the people in his tribe or band. In all the Plains Indian tribes, an individual warrior could make decisions for himself only; therefore, not only did the federal government fail to live up to terms of the treaty, but Indians didn't feel bound by it either.

Nevertheless, the 1851 Treaty of Fort Laramie did allow for fairly unrestricted travel over the emigrant trails for the next ten years. Not until the early 1860s did hostilities along the trails escalate, and then it did so because of increasing encroachment into Indian territories in Colorado, Nebraska, and eventually northeastern Wyoming.

Fort Laramie Treaty, 1868 ▣ Å

A second major treaty with Plains Indians was negotiated at Fort Laramie in 1868, culminating in the end of the four-year Northern Plains War, which became known as Red Cloud's War. The treaty was with various tribal factions, the most important of them led by Oglala Lakota chief Red Cloud. It also involved bands from the Brulé, Oglala, Miniconjou, Yanktonai, Hunkpapa, Blackfeet, Cuthead, Two Kettle, Sans Arcs, Santee, and Arapaho tribes. This treaty, concluded on April 29, 1868, called for abandonment of the Bozeman Trail forts: Fort Reno, Fort Phil Kearny, and Fort C. F. Smith. The military did not officially abandon the forts until later that summer; Indians burned all three immediately.

The terms of the 1868 treaty established the Great Sioux Reservation, covering the western half of South Dakota. Hunting privileges were extended to the tribes on any lands north of the Platte River in Wyoming Territory and on the Republican Fork of the Smoky Hill River in Colorado Territory "so long as the buffalo may range thereon in such numbers as to justify the chase" (Treaty with the Sioux 1868, Article 11).

The treaty stated that the land east of the Big Horn Mountains and north of the North Platte River in Wyoming was "unceded" and, therefore, reserved for the tribes (Article 16).

The treaty provided for the annual distribution of clothing for Lakota tribal members (Article 10), establishment of an agency that would be managed by a government-appointed agent (Article 5), and construction on the reservation of various buildings, including a "good steam circular-saw mill" with a grist mill and shingle mill attached, a schoolhouse, residences for the agent and a physician, and buildings for "a carpenter, farmer, blacksmith, miller, and engineer" (Article 4).

In exchange, the Indians agreed not to oppose construction of railroads, roads, mail stations, or "other works of utility" passing through their lands. Also, they were expected to withdraw opposition to military posts then established—or that could be built in the future—south of the North Platte River (Article 11).

Other treaties made at Fort Laramie in 1868 included one with the Crows and another involving the Northern Cheyennes and Northern Arapahos.

Fort Mackenzie 🚩 🏳️
Sheridan County

Named for General Ranald S. Mackenzie, who had fought with Crook in various campaigns in Wyoming, Fort Mackenzie was authorized by Congress based on an 1889 recommendation by General Edwin V. Sumner to establish a military post in the area to protect settlers. The red brick buildings of the fort were constructed in 1902. The Second and Third Battalions of the U.S. Eighteenth Infantry were stationed at the post in 1909. They were transferred to Texas in 1911, and only caretakers remained at Fort Mackenzie, which was abandoned in 1918. The post buildings are now part of a veterans' hospital in Sheridan.

Fort McGraw 🏴
Fremont County
(*See* Camp McGraw.)

Fort McKinney 🏴 🏴
Johnson County

Two posts went by the same name, both in Johnson County. The first was known initially as Cantonment Reno (*see entry*) and then became Fort McKinney for Lieutenant John A. McKinney, one of the soldiers who died in the November 25, 1876, Dull Knife battle. That post was later renamed Depot McKinney when a newer fort called Fort McKinney was established at a location farther west just on the outskirts of present Buffalo.

Troops from Fort McKinney patrolled to be certain that Indians remained on their reservations. They also provided protection for stages running through the area on the Rock Creek to Terry's Landing route—Rock Creek is in southern Wyoming and Terry's Landing is on the Yellowstone River in present Montana. In 1892, troops from Fort McKinney rode south to the TA Ranch to take into custody the men who had invaded Johnson County in a conflict with homesteaders/rustlers. They held the invaders, or Regulators as they were called, for a time at Fort McKinney then accompanied them to Cheyenne for a planned trial, although the charges were eventually dismissed. (*See also* Johnson County Invasion/War.)

Fort McKinney's facilities were abandoned by the military in 1895 and turned over to the state of Wyoming in 1903. They are now the site of the Wyoming Veterans' Home off U.S. 16 at the western edge of Buffalo.

Fort Nonsense
Sublette County
(*See* Fort Bonneville.)

Fort Platte 🏴 🚂
Goshen County

In 1839, Lancaster P. Lupton, a fur trader who also had built a fort on the South Platte River in Colorado, started construction of this adobe-walled post, also called Richard's Fort, very near Fort Laramie. Though it was not complete, it opened for business. Then in 1841 it was sold to Sybille, Adams & Company, and in 1843, it was owned by Pratte & Cabanne (Haines 1981). The post had about a dozen buildings, including a warehouse, store, office, carpenter shop, kitchen, and dwellings, along with a large corral. In 1842 explorer Lieutenant John C. Frémont described it as "built of earth, and still unfinished, being enclosed with walls, or rather houses, on three of the sides, and open on the fourth to the river" (Jackson & Spence 1970, as quoted in Haines 1981, 128).

By 1845 the post was abandoned, and in 1849 California Trail traveler J. Goldsborough Bruff passed the site, writing, "Several hundred yards back from the river's bank, on the right, stood the old adobe walls of Fort Platte . . . now in ruins; and looks like an old Castle. It is rectangular" (Bruff 1949, as quoted in Haines 1981, 128). The site was two miles west of the town of Fort Laramie on the road to Fort Laramie National Historic Site.

Fort Reno 🖅 🏴
Johnson County

Named for Major Jesse L. Reno, who died September 14, 1862, at the Battle of South Mountain in Maryland during the Civil War, this fort was west of Pumpkin Buttes on the Powder River about twenty-two miles northeast of present Kaycee. It was constructed in 1865 to protect travelers on the Bozeman Trail. Established August 14, 1865, by Brigadier General Patrick E. Connor, it was initially known as Camp or Fort Connor but later renamed Fort Reno.

The post first had a rough stockade surrounding the warehouse and stables. Initially the quarters for both officers and enlisted men were unprotected, but in 1866 Colonel H. B. Carrington reconstructed the post at a new nearby location, adding better buildings and a stockade that included blockhouses with bastions on opposite corners.

Among the troops at the fort were the Sixth Michigan Cavalry under the command of Colonel James H. Kidd and two companies of the Nineteenth U. S. Infantry led by Captain Joseph L. Proctor. Proctor had troops enlarge the facility significantly (Frazier 1972).

Fort Reno, established on Powder River in 1865, was first called Camp or Fort Connor, but it was later rebuilt and renamed Fort Reno by Colonel H. B. Carrington. (*Courtesy Wyoming State Museum*)

Fort Reno was abandoned under provisions of the April 29, 1868, Fort Laramie Treaty and subsequently burned by Indians.

Fort Riley to Bridger's Pass Road
Laramie, Albany, and Carbon Counties

Lieutenant F. T. Bryan left Fort Riley, Kansas, on June 21, 1856, on an expedition to determine a route for a road connecting Fort Riley, Kansas, with Bridger's Pass, which was then in Nebraska Territory but is currently in Carbon County, Wyoming. Accompanying Bryan were John Lambert, topographer; Henry Englemann, geologist; Charles Larned, in charge of barometers; and two rodmen. Accompanied by a military escort, the expedition had thirty-three wagons.

In Wyoming their route passed near present Pine Bluffs, Cheyenne, Laramie, Elk Mountain, and south of Rawlins. A report by Bryan outlined the country and its resources. Bryan's official report reads as follows:

> Tuesday, August 5.—Our route for today was across the plains from the east to the west fork of Laramie [Big and

Little Laramie rivers], a distance of fifteen miles. Camped on the right bank of the west fork, a beautiful mountain stream, flowing from the Medicine-Bon [Medicine Bow] mountains; on our left over a fine, hard bed of gravel and pebbles. The water is clear and of an icy coldness.

Wednesday, August 6.—Today crossed the west fork without difficulty, and in about a mile struck into the emigrant road [Cherokee Trail] along the foot of the Medicine-Bon [Bow]. . . . The road today is very good, having occasional ascents and descents, and over a fine, hard gravel; it is, however, very destructive to the feet of our animals, many of them losing their shoes, and becoming tender footed in consequence. Trains traveling through this country should be well provided with those indispensable article[s], horse and mule shoes, and shoe nails, as many are worn out and lost. A forge would be necessary for a large train. Camped after a march of fourteen miles on a small creek of good water. This we called Cooper's creek. . . .

Monday, August 11, 1856.—Crossing the creek, we followed an Indian trail leading down the right bank [of Pass Creek on the south side of Elk Mountain], until the hills came so close to the creek that we were obliged to take to the road [Cherokee Trail] again. This we had avoided as much as possible today, as it led over a succession of ascents and descents. Even after we entered the road again we were obliged, for about three miles, to make our way almost at right angles across the spurs coming down from Medicine-Bon butte [Elk Mountain] on our right. In some places the road ran over side hills so steep that it was necessary to hold up the wagons with ropes. Two wagons overturned in making the passage. This three or four miles through the canon of Pass creek would require a good deal of work, a week's work for a company. The road should follow the creek more closely than the present one does. . . . (Bryan 1857, as quoted in *Annals of Wyoming* 1945, 30–31).

Fort D. A. Russell 🚩 🏴 🚂
Laramie County

The location of this fort, selected by Commander of the Twelfth U.S. Infantry General Christopher C. Augur on July 4, 1867, to protect workers building the Union Pacific Railroad, was on Crow Creek three miles west of Cheyenne.

Colonel John D. Stevenson, Thirtieth U.S. Infantry, established the post, which is named for Eighth U.S. Infantry Brigadier General David A. Russell, who died September 19, 1864, in the Battle of Opequon, Virginia.

The garrison included detachments from the Second U.S. Cavalry and the Thirtieth U.S. Infantry, whose members first lived in tents and log huts. During the winter of 1867–1868, both officers and enlisted men constructed quarters of wood frame design situated in a diamond-shaped pattern that opened to the east.

Fort Russell was supported by Camp Carlin, which served as a supply depot during construction of the Union Pacific Railroad and later during the Indian Wars. It was officially known as Cheyenne Depot. Fort Russell became permanent in 1885 under orders from the U.S. War Department, and at that time it was rebuilt to house eight companies of infantry adequately. During the Spanish-American War, it was the mobilization center for the Wyoming National Guard. It had a similar role for both cavalry and field artillery during World War I.

Fort D. A. Russell was renamed Fort Francis E. Warren on January 1, 1930, for a prominent Wyoming resident and former governor. Still in use, the fort was taken over by the U.S. Air Force in 1947 to serve as a training center and renamed Fort Francis E. Warren Air Force Base. In 1963 F. E. Warren AFB became part of the Strategic Air Command, Ninetieth Strategic Wing, housing Minuteman Missiles. It remains in use by the U.S. Air Force.

Fort Sanders 🚩 🏴 🛻 🚂
Albany County

First known as Fort John Buford (*see entry*), this post south of the present city of Laramie was renamed Fort Sanders on September 5,

The Fort Sanders guardhouse stands at the south edge of Laramie. (*Courtesy Wyoming State Preservation Office*)

1866, for Brigadier General William P. Sanders, who died of his Civil War battle wounds on November 19, 1863. The fort stood on a military reservation nine miles square and included facilities to house six companies of soldiers. The purpose of Fort Sanders was to provide protection for travelers on the Lodgepole Trail and the Overland Trail, which converged at the fort's location. It also provided protection for the stage route between Denver and Salt Lake City and later for survey and construction crews involved in building the transcontinental railroad. A telegraph office was established at the fort in 1867.

Fort Sanders had three quartermaster houses, three commissary stores, a sawmill, a blacksmith shop, a shoemaker, thirteen sets of wash and laundry quarters, and stables for the cavalry horses. A hospital was constructed initially of logs, then frame construction was added (Carley 1961a). The post was abandoned May 22, 1882.

It was at Fort Sanders that the first newspaper in Wyoming was printed. An enterprising editor had his equipment set up inside a Union Pacific train car, and while it was stopped at Fort Sanders, he composed and printed the first issue of the *Frontier Index* in Wyoming. The paper itself had started in Fort Kearny, Nebraska, in 1867 and was published by Leigh Freeman and his brother at varying locations along the route of the Union Pacific Railroad, including Cheyenne, Fort Sanders, Green River City, and Bear River City. The Freeman brothers continued traveling west with the railroad and published additional issues in Utah. The last known issue of the paper is dated November 17, 1868. The Freeman brothers went on to publish other newspapers in Utah.

Fort Stambaugh 🚩 📧
Fremont County
(*See* Camp Stambaugh.)

Fort Fred Steele 🚩 📧 🚂
Carbon County
Fort Fred Steele was located on the west bank of the North Platte River near the Union Pacific Railroad line and just north of present Interstate 80 and the Fort Steele Rest Area. Named for Captain Frederick Steele, Twentieth U.S. Infantry, who died January 12, 1868, when he fell from a carriage, Fort Fred Steele was established June 30, 1868, to protect Union Pacific tracklayers.

Two decades earlier, in 1843, Lieutenant John C. Frémont had an encounter with Cheyenne and Arapaho Indians in the vicinity. The Frémont party had set up a camp, having killed some buffalo and intending to preserve the meat. The men built scaffolds for that purpose, but then around seventy Indians attacked. Frémont's men countered with gunfire, but when the Indians realized it was a military party and not a band of enemy warriors, the fight stopped, and the two sides then exchanged gifts.

The fort was located on a thirty-six square-mile military reservation with most buildings constructed of logs hauled in from Elk Mountain or floated down the North Platte River from camps in the Sierra Madre Range about forty miles to the south. A fort sawmill operated by Barton T. Ryan turned the raw timber into lumber for various structures, and a large number of tents were used for accommodations for men.

Fort Fred Steele had adequate quarters for five companies of soldiers. Buildings also included a library, a storehouse for the quartermaster and commissary, stables, shops for carpenters, a blacksmith, a bakery, a granary, and an area for laundresses. Once the Union Pacific Railroad was in place, the fort was a strategic supply location. The area also remained a target for raiding Indians.

It was from Fort Fred Steele that troops under command of Colonel Thomas Tipton Thornburgh rode in September 1879 upon request for military intervention on the White River Reservation near present Meeker, Colorado. White River Indian Agent, Nathan C. Meeker, concerned about increasing unrest among Ute Indians, sought the military assistance. Thornburgh's command, as part of the White River Expedition, crossed onto the Indian reservation near Milk Creek, south of Craig, Colorado, and engaged in a fierce battle with Utes that led to a siege and the death of Thornburgh and many of his men. At the same time, other Utes attacked at the White River Agency, killing Meeker and several of the men there before taking Meeker's wife, Arvilla, and daughter, Josephine, plus another woman and two children as hostages.

Soon after the September 29 battle at Milk Creek, Joe Rankin, a Rawlins livery station owner and scout for Thornburgh's command (who later became a U. S. marshal), left the besieged military camp and rode some 150 miles in slightly more than twenty-seven hours to Rawlins where he sent word to military authorities of the attack. Rawlins was the most significant community in the vicinity with both a telegraph and access to rail transportation for relief troops. A military expedition commanded by General Wesley Merritt quickly organized at Fort D. A. Russell before taking a train to Rawlins and then marching south to Milk Creek and eventually to the White River Agency itself. The Utes subsequently released the hostages.

Fort Fred Steele was abandoned in the fall of 1886. Most troops had departed by November 3. Some buildings from the fort era remain at Fort Fred Steele, which is now a Wyoming State Historical Site located near the highway rest area of the same name.

Fort Supply 🖅 🚂
Uinta County
Located about a dozen miles southwest of Fort Bridger, Fort Supply served Mormons from 1853 until 1857. The Mormons burned the structures before they retreated to Utah in 1857 ahead of federal troops commanded by Colonel Albert Sidney Johnston. (*See* Utah War of 1857.)

Fort Thompson 🖅 🏴
Fremont County
In use from 1857 through 1858 as the U. S. Army marched toward Utah, this fort was on the Popo Agie River, near present Lander (Urbanek 1990).

Fort Walbach 🏴
Laramie County
(*See* Camp Walbach.)

Fort Francis E. Warren 🖅 🏴
Laramie County
(*See* Fort D. A. Russell.)

Fort Washakie 🖅 🏴 ⚠
Fremont County
The Shoshone Indians agreed to settle on a reservation in the Wind River Basin in 1863, but after attacks by enemy tribes, including the Arapahos, Cheyennes, and Sioux, Chief Washakie of the Shoshones took his people off of the eastern portion of the reservation and said he would not return without protection. The Shoshones roamed throughout western Wyoming until 1868 when Washakie learned that the Bannocks were to receive a new reservation farther west in Idaho. At the time, Washakie realized he would not be able to hold onto his entire homeland, so at a treaty conference at Fort Bridger, he negotiated for what he considered the best portion of it: 601,120 acres of fertile river country in the Wind River Basin. He also demanded protection from enemies of the Shoshones.

The government stationed troops at Fort Brown and established an Indian police force as well. Originally called Camp Augur, then Camp Brown or Fort Brown, the post was renamed Fort Washakie for the Shoshone Chief in 1878 when it was relocated to a new site closer to the Indian Agency. That year Captain Robert A. Torrey, Thirteenth U. S. Infantry, had taken over command of Camp Brown, and he selected the new site for the post. The new military post was officially established June 26, 1871, near the confluence of the North and South Forks of the Little Wind River. The name of the post was changed to Fort Washakie on December 30, 1878. It had a military presence from 1870 through 1909.

An order of abandonment of the post was issued in 1899, but Chief Washakie objected strenuously, and the fort remained in use through May 1, 1907, when army troops left the area. But Fort Washakie was reopened, and by October 14, 1907, it was again considered a permanent military post until it was abandoned finally on March 30, 1909.

When first built, the post had company barracks, a mess hall, a kitchen, a bakery, officers' quarters, a guardhouse, and a reading room. Other buildings served as storehouses, laundresses' quarters, and stables. The buildings were constructed of both adobe and logs; most had sod roofs. The post also had corrals. In 1872, a large storehouse and a small building used as a hospital were added to the facilities. Around 1885 more construction took place with materials such as sandstone used for several buildings, some of which are still standing and in use for various purposes in the community of Fort Washakie, which remains the headquarters for the Eastern Shoshone tribe. (*See also* Fort Brown.)

Fort William 🛶 🚂
Goshen County
This trading post was constructed near the Laramie River by Robert Campbell and William Sublette in 1834. It predated Fort John and Fort Laramie, which were in the same general area. Fort William was constructed of hewn cottonwood logs with fifteen-foot bastioned walls around an area that was eighty by one hundred feet. Used mainly to serve fur traders, Fort William, located about two

miles west of the present town of Fort Laramie, was sold in 1835 to Jim Bridger, Thomas Fitzpatrick, and Milton G. Sublette, one of William Sublette's brothers, who transferred ownership to the American Fur Company in 1836. By 1838 Pierre Chouteau, Jr. & Company owned and operated it. (*See also* Fort Laramie.)

Fort Yellowstone 🚩 🏴
Yellowstone National Park

Captain Moses Harris, First U. S. Cavalry, established this post August 17, 1886, near Mammoth Hot Springs in Yellowstone National Park. The role of the troops stationed at the fort was to enforce game laws and protect park sites. The fort was initially known as Camp Sheridan, for Lieutenant General Phil Sheridan, but was redesignated as Fort Yellowstone on May 11, 1891. The fort was abandoned as a military post in 1918, but many of the buildings remain in use as park headquarters and for other operations at Mammoth Village. There is a self-guided historic walking tour of the fort grounds. Park management now falls under the jurisdiction of the Department of the Interior/National Park Service.

Fremont Canyon 🌲 🛶
Natrona County

Named for explorer Lieutenant John Charles Frémont, who first saw the white water of the North Platte River in this canyon in 1842, Fremont Canyon was first called "Fiery Narrows." It is now downstream from Pathfinder Reservoir, twenty miles west of Casper, so water flows are not as wild as they were when Frémont visited the area. In his journal of the 1842 trip, Frémont writes:

> We found this passage much worse than the previous one, and our position was rather a bad one. To go back, was impossible, before us, the cataract was a sheet of foam; and, shut up in the chasm by the rocks, which in some places seemed almost to meet overhead, the roar of the water was deafening (Frémont 1842, as quoted in Wyoming Recreation Commission 1988, 169).

Frémont Expeditions, 1842 and 1844 🦅 🏴

Lieutenant John Charles Frémont first made his way through Wyoming on his 1842 exploration of the West, and he returned to the region in 1844. Tom Fitzpatrick and Kit Carson served as guides on the latter journey, and it was during that trip that Frémont traversed the Sierra Madre Range, providing the first official government report on the region.

On June 13, 1844, Frémont was at the north end of the Sierra Madres, writing the following, which became part of his official report to Congress in 1845:

> Issuing from the pines in the afternoon, we saw spread out before us the valley of the Platte, with the pass of the Medicine Butte [Elk Mountain] beyond, and some of the Sweet Water mountains; but a smoky haziness in the air entirely obscured the Wind River Chain (1845, 281).[3]

The party then turned south, skirting the east face of the Sierra Madre Range, where the next day, Frémont added the following to his report:

> June 14.—Our route this morning lay along the foot of the mountains, over the long low spurs which sloped gradually down to the river, forming the broad valley of the [North] Platte. The country is beautifully watered. In almost every hollow ran a clear, cool mountain stream; and in the course of the morning we crossed seventeen, several of them being large creeks, forty to fifty feet wide, with a swift current, and tolerable deep. These were variously wooded with groves of aspen and cottonwood, with willow, cherry, and other shrubby trees. Buffalo, antelope, and elk were frequent during the day. . . .
>
> We halted at noon on Potter's fork [Encampment River near Riverside]—a clear and swift stream, forty yards wide, and in many places deep enough to swim our animals . . . (Frémont 1845, 281).

Gilbert's Station 🛒
Fremont County

Another name for Burnt Ranch (*see entry*), Gilbert's Station was one point from which travelers who took the Pacific Road or Lander Road to Oregon departed from the main trail west.

Glenrock 🚂 🛒
Converse County

Known by emigrants as Rock in the Glen, this major campsite on the Oregon–California road was at the location of the present town of Glenrock. By 1850 Mormons had established a way station at the site that they maintained until abandoning it in the face of an oncoming U.S. Army led by Colonel Albert Sidney Johnston in 1857 during the so-called "Mormon War" (*see* Utah War of 1857). Indian Agent Thomas Twiss relocated his agency (without official permission) from Fort Laramie to Deer Creek, about four miles upstream from the confluence with the North Platte River, calling the new site Upper Platte River Indian Agency.

In 1859 Twiss recommended a treaty with Indians that would establish a reservation system and specific territories for the various tribes. A formal treaty with the tribes, including the Brulé and Oglala Sioux, the Arapaho, and the Cheyenne, was negotiated by September 18, 1859. Among its provisions: land along Deer Creek would have been set aside for the Sioux. Congress never ratified the treaty. Like some other Indian agents, Twiss was not particularly reliable, and when he eventually resigned his position, the Upper Platte River Agency was relocated back near Fort Laramie.

This station also served the Pony Express operators who called it Rock in the Glen, Glen Rock Station, or Little Muddy Station.

Grand Encampment 🛶
Carbon County

In 1838, on the banks of a stream they knew as Potter's Fork, fur trappers held a small rendezvous and called the site Camp le Grande. It later became Grand Encampment, the name it was incorporated under after a copper boom in 1897 attracted thousands to the area.

Ben Kern, wagon master of the 2007 Overland Trail Wagon Train, drove the Wyoming State Parks stagecoach to Granger Station. (*Candy Moulton*)

Grand Encampment Stage Line 🚂
Carbon County
George Nuzum operated this stage line, which served miners and other travelers with terminal points at Grand Encampment and Walcott. The line was in use from shortly after the discovery of copper in the Grand Encampment Copper District in 1897 until 1903 when it was purchased by Charles M. Scribner. (*See also* Short Line Stage Company and Lake Creek Stage Station.)

Granger Stage Station 🚂
Sweetwater County
This station at the southeastern edge of the town of Granger served traffic on the Oregon and Overland Trail (which overlapped in this area) and went by the names Granger Station, Ham's Fork Station, and South Bend Station. The chronology of the names for the station is not clear, though it appears to have been called Ham's Fork or Granger Station before 1867 and South Bend Station after that time,

A wagon train following the Overland Trail in 2007 stopped at the Granger Station. (*Candy Moulton*)

when it was so listed on the timetable that Wells, Fargo Company coaches used. Bureau of Land Management Archaeologist Russ Tanner notes in his 1984 report "The Controversy Surrounding the Granger Stage Station, Wyoming" that the name switch to Granger could have taken place in 1868 for the first postmaster in the area, Lafayette Granger. The post office began operating in February 1869.

The station served traffic on the Oregon Trail, was a Pony Express stop in 1860 and 1861, and in 1862 became a regular stop on Ben Holladay's Overland Stage Line.

Gratiot Houses
Goshen County

Little is known about this trading post, apparently comprising several structures or houses and located about three and one-half miles southeast of Fort Laramie. Reportedly, it was plundered by Indians after the Grattan Massacre that occurred nearby.

Grattan Massacre 🚩 🏳️ 🏕️
Goshen County

A footsore cow left along the trail by a Mormon party precipitated the first violent encounter in Wyoming between the frontier military and the Lakota Indians. The cow, left on the trail in mid-August 1854, was subsequently found by a Lakota from the Miniconjou band. The Indian killed the cow, and the people he was traveling with ate the animal. Shortly thereafter the Mormon who had owned the cow lodged a complaint with officials at Fort Laramie.

At the time a fairly large contingent of Indians was camped near Fort Laramie, awaiting supplies that were to be delivered under provisions of the 1851 treaty. They expected to get the supplies at the Gratiot Houses. When the Indians found out the Mormon protested the loss of his cow, they tried to make restitution, but officials at the fort turned them away. Subsequently, a military company of twenty-five privates, two musicians, and a civilian interpreter, Lucien Auguste, headed to the camp where High Forehead, the Indian who had taken and killed the cow, was staying. Led by Second Lieutenant John L. Grattan, the military party entered the Indian camp of Conquering Bear. Initially discussions were cordial, but when the military attempted to arrest High Forehead, someone fired a shot, and the camp erupted in violence.

Some of the soldiers escaped the Indian camp after the first volley of fire, although they were soon followed and killed by the Indians. One private managed to elude the Indians for a time and, though wounded, made his way back to Fort Laramie. He died at the fort after telling of the incident that had taken the lives of all of Grattan's men and the lieutenant himself.

Trader James Bordeaux, who was in the Indian camp that day, and Lakota Chief Man-Afraid-Of-His-Horses both later said the incident escalated in large part because interpreter Auguste was drunk.

There was no immediate retaliation against the Indians, but the frontier military took action the following August in present Nebraska by attacking and killing many Indians in a fight that became known as the Battle of Blue Water or the Harney Massacre. The Indians attacked in that 1855 battle were not the same band that had been involved in the Grattan Massacre, as the 1854 incident quickly became known. Because of the Grattan Massacre, however, there were subsequent hostilities involving Indians and military troops all along the overland trail corridor.

The site where the Grattan Massacre occurred is now a field about seven miles southeast of Fort Laramie accessible via dirt roads. For directions, contact the Fort Laramie National Historic Site.

Green River Expedition 🛶
Sweetwater County

After spending the winter of 1868–1869 in western Colorado near present Meeker, Major John Wesley Powell and his men, known as The Rocky Mountain Scientific Exploring Expedition, reached Green River City, a terminus of the Union Pacific Railroad, where they launched their first expedition down the Green and Colorado Rivers. Powell writes on May 24, 1869:

> The good people of Green River City turn out to see us start. We raise our little flag, push the boats from the shore, and the swift current carries us down. Our boats are four in number. . . . We take with us rations deemed sufficient to last ten months (Crutchfied 1993, 57).

This first expedition started with four boats—the *Kitty Clyde's Sister*, *No Name*, *Maid of the Cañon*, and *Emma Dean*, the last, the smallest of the crafts, named for Powell's wife. Powell floated the Green River south out of Wyoming and across Brown's Hole (he called it Brown's Park and the name stuck) before entering the canyon he called Lodore, named for the Robert Southey poem "The Cataract of Lodore." Here the crew in the *No Name* missed a signal from Powell and plunged into the canyon. They dropped over a short waterfall, smacked a rock, cracked their boat in two, and were tossed into the raging river. Although the men survived, their boat and the supplies and scientific instruments in it did not. They had lost guns and maps, notes from their trip, and all the clothing they had brought except what they were wearing. It was the first of many dangerous, potentially deadly, incidents they faced as they journeyed from Green River to the Grand Canyon.

The 2007 Overland Trail Wagon Train crosses the Green River downstream from the commonly used trail era crossing points. (*Candy Moulton*)

Powell was at the mouth of the Grand Canyon August 13, 1869, ready to start his way down what he termed "the Great Unknown." The party split near the south end of Grand Canyon. Some of the men left the river and continued overland, where they were attacked and killed by Indians. The remainder, now too few to man all three boats, abandoned the *Emma Dean*. The following day—after two weeks within its confines—they broke free of the canyon and entered the Grand Wash. Continuing downstream, they arrived at the confluence of the Virgin River on August 30 and were greeted by Mormon settlers, sixty-nine days after they had pushed their boats into the water at Green River City.

Two years later, on May 22, 1871, Powell was back in Green River City, launching his second exploratory trip down the Green River. (*See also* Expedition Island.)

Green River Station 🚏 🚃
Sweetwater County
This station was located where the Overland Trail crossed the Green River just west of the town of Green River. During low water, wagons could ford the Green River, but at other times a ferry operated.

The station also served the Pony Express as a home station in 1860 and 1861. Sir Richard Burton describes it thus:

> The station was the home of Mc. Macarthy, our driver. . . . We supped comfortable at Green-River Station, the stream supplying excellent salmon-trout [likely Colorado cutthroat trout]. The kichimichi, or buffalo-berry, makes tolerable jelly, and alongside of the station is a store where Mr. Burton (of Maine) sells "Valley Tan" whiskey (1862; reprint 1990, 170).

Greenwood Cutoff, California Trail 🛒
Sublette County

Mountain man Caleb Greenwood was eighty-one years old in 1844 when the westbound Stevens–Townsend–Murphy wagon train reached present southwest Wyoming. Those travelers wanted a faster route to California than the route via Fort Bridger, so Greenwood took them over a route that headed almost due west from a point about four miles north of present Farson to cross the Green River near Names Hill, located adjacent to U.S. 189 south of LaBarge. By taking the route, travelers did not go south to Fort Bridger before turning back to the northwest so they saved considerable miles of travel. The drawback, however, was the route had no water. As a result most people who followed Greenwood's Cutoff generally left from their last camp where they had water late in the afternoon and traveled all night so they could reach the Green River before the main heat of the following day. The crossing was about forty miles, making it one of the longest single-day drives most emigrants undertook.

In 1849 Joseph E. Ware prepared a guidebook that included information about the Greenwood Cutoff. He called the route the Sublette Cutoff, for the Sublette brothers who had been trappers in the region since the 1820s. As a result the route is now most often called the Sublette Cutoff (*see entry*).

Guernsey Ruts, Oregon–California Trail 🚩 🛒
Platte County

Located a mile and a half southeast of Guernsey on road 109S, the deep ruts carved in sandstone above the North Platte River were first made by emigrants traveling the Oregon–California road. The wagons pulled away from the river valley, as the present road goes, and climbed over the rugged hills because the valley area was marshy during the period of trail travel. Although the ruts initially came from emigrant wagons, the deep cut now visible was enhanced by heavily laden wagons hauling building materials to Fort Laramie after the period of emigrant wagon trains. The ruts at Guernsey are now a Wyoming State Historic Site. They are also identified as Oregon Trail Ruts and referred to as Deep Rut Hill.

Guinard's Bridge
Natrona County

In 1858 Louis Guinard built a thirteen-foot-wide log bridge across the North Platte River at the site the Mormon Ferry had operated from 1847 to 1852. The bridge was near the present Fort Caspar Historic Site in the city of Casper. Guinard charged a toll to use his bridge. As Sir Richard Burton notes: "[T]he usual toll is $0.50, but from trains, especially Mormons, the owner will claim $5; in fact, as much as he can get without driving them to the opposition lower bridge [Richard/Reshaw], or to the ferry boat" (1862; reprint 1990, 141).

Guinard's bridge remained in place for use by travelers until 1867 when troops abandoned Fort Caspar. At that time Indians burned the bridge.

Halter and Flick Ranch
Sweetwater County

This is a later name for the Pacific Springs Stage Station (*see entry*), though the buildings remaining are remnants of a brothel and gambling establishment. It is on private land off Wyoming Highway 28 about twenty-five miles east of Farson.

Ham's Fork Station
Sweetwater County

Also called South Bend Station and Granger Stage Station (*see entries*), this station served the Overland Trail as a home station and site of a telegraph office. Constructed of sandstone blocks, it stood near the confluence of the Ham's Fork and Black's Fork Rivers.

Travelers visit Hat Creek Station in 1875. (*Courtesy Wyoming State Archives*)

Hat Creek Station 🚂 🚃
Niobrara County

John Bowman and Joe Walters started Hat Creek Ranch in 1876, turning it into a stage stop on the Cheyenne–Deadwood stage route. When their first building burned in 1883, they replaced it with a two-story log structure that still stands thirteen miles north of Lusk near U.S. 85. At various times Hat Creek Station served as a telegraph station, post office, hotel, and blacksmith shop. Here in 1877, Crazy Horse surrendered to military officials as he made the transition from free-ranging warrior to reservation Indian.

In July 1876 an army camp was at the site. In an April 1877 article in *Scribner's Monthly*, Leander P. Richardson writes:

> Just across the creek was a soldiers' camp garrisoned by six men. The regular number kept at the Hat Creek camp is from forty to forty-five, but the majority of the soldiers were now away on a scouting expedition with General [Wesley M.] Merritt. Close beside the camp is a building ordinarily known as "Johnny Bowman's Ranch." These ranches, which abound along the lines of all of the stage and freight roads in this wilderness, form a peculiar phase of frontier life. They are hotels, bar-rooms and stores for general merchandise, all combined in one, and the whole business is

usually transacted in a single room. At any of these places a traveler can purchase almost anything, from a glass of whiskey to a four-horse team, but the former is usually the staple of demand (Richardson 1877, as quoted in McFarling 1955, 36–37).

Joel Hembree Grave 🚏 🛻
Converse County
This grave beside LaPrele Creek, northwest of Douglas, holds Joel Hembree, the first person to die on the "Great Migration" over the Oregon Trail in 1843. The six-year-old boy died when he fell from a wagon and it ran over him. (*See also* LaPrele Station.)

Hoback Canyon 🌲 🛶
Teton County
Trapper John Hoback and companions Edward Robinson and Jacob Reznor guided sixty-one Astorians, who were members of the American Fur Company, through northwest Wyoming in 1811. The party included Pierre Dorion, Jr. and his Indian wife, Marie, plus their two young sons. At a site twenty-eight miles north of present-day Pinedale, and near Wyoming Highway 189/191, the Astorians camped before resuming their trek through the canyon carved by the Snake River that mountain men called the Mad River. The canyon subsequently took Hoback's name.

Hole-in-the-Wall 🌲
Johnson County
A hideout for outlaws and train robbers as well as cattle rustlers, the Hole-in-the-Wall country gets its name for a break in the red wall leading toward the east and Powder River Basin. The trail to the hole is steep and winding, barely wide enough for a horse and rider, but through it went such men as Butch Cassidy, Flat Nose George Currie, and Harry "Sundance Kid" Longabaugh (sometimes spelled Longbaugh), not to mention unnamed and uncounted cattle thieves. The hole-in-the-wall itself is west of Kaycee on public land managed by the Bureau of Land Management, but access to it is easiest by

crossing private ranch lands. Therefore, the best way to visit the hole is to contact Willow Creek Ranch, which offers tours of the area.

Horse Creek Station
Natrona County

When a stage station was established at this stream about twelve miles northeast of Independence Rock off Wyoming Highway 220 between Casper and Rawlins, the creek that had been known as Greasewood Creek was renamed Horse Creek. Some emigrants also called it Sage Creek because of the abundant amount of brush that could be used for firewood. It was likely near this site in 1856 that the first wave of rescuers found the Edward Martin Mormon handcart party. Because those first rescuers had few supplies, they encouraged the Martin party members to pick up their handcarts and continue moving west to Sweetwater Station to what eventually became Martin's Cove (*see* Martin's Cove and Sweetwater Station entries). The station also served the Pony Express in 1860 and 1861.

Horseshoe Creek, Battle of
Platte County

This battle between men at Horseshoe Station and Oglala and Miniconjou warriors took place March 19–21, 1868. (*See also* Horseshoe Station.)

Horseshoe Station
Platte County

Located about two miles south of present Glendo on Horseshoe Creek, this station was one of several the Mormons established to provide supplies and support for thousands of followers of the Church of Jesus Christ of Latter-day Saints who migrated west beginning in 1847.

In 1856 when Hiram Kimball's Mormon Mail Service received the contract to carry the U.S. mail between Fort Laramie and Salt Lake City, the site expanded to include a stage station. It also served travelers on the Oregon–California Road. The Mormon complex comprised 640 acres, where the Mormons raised crops and kept around 75 horses and 125 oxen. An area for thirty or forty houses with gardens was near the creek. The Mormons abandoned the station in 1857 as they retreated in advance of troops led by Colonel Albert Sidney Johnston during his push to Utah for the anticipated "Mormon War" (*see* Utah War of 1857). A fire burned the deserted buildings in October 1857.

Horseshoe Station was reestablished either on or near this site by 1860 when Russell, Majors, and Waddell organized their Pony Express service. For a time the notorious Jack Slade was division-agent with headquarters here. The location served as a telegraph station beginning in 1861. Slade hired 14-year-old Buffalo Bill Cody as a Pony Express rider at Horseshoe Station, according to Cody's autobiography, and Mark Twain wrote about his encounter with Slade, which most likely was at Horseshoe Station, in his book *Roughing It*.

An attack on Horseshoe Station in mid-March 1868 by Oglala and Miniconjou warriors may have been led by Crazy Horse. The men from the station abandoned the post after Indians set fire to the buildings. Subsequent fighting took place in a running battle between Horseshoe Station and Diamond A Hill. The men first holed-up at Mouseau's Road Ranch near Twin Springs, eventually fleeing toward Fort Laramie after burning Mouseau's to keep it from falling into Indian hands. After three days and fatalities on both sides, an agreement made between the parties ended the fighting. (*See also* Portugee Phillips' Ride and Fetterman Fight.)

Ice Slough Station ⌇ 🛖
Fremont County

Ice Slough, adjacent to U. S. 287 about eight miles north of Jeffrey City, was a recognized point on the Oregon Trail, known for the peaty bog that protected an ice field where emigrants could dig down and get ice even during the middle of summer. (Trail guidebooks provided useful information about locations such as Ice Slough to travelers.) During 1860 and 1861, the site served as a Pony Express relay station.

Independence Rock ⌇ 🌲 🛖
Natrona County

The most recognized landmark on the Oregon–California Trail across Wyoming is Independence Rock, a unique granite outcrop beside the

William Henry Jackson's depicted wagon train travel on the Oregon Trail near Independence Rock, with Devil's Gate in the background. (*National Park Service Photo*)

Sweetwater River located midway between Casper and Rawlins along Wyoming Highway 220. According to legend, the rock received its name in 1830 when a party of trappers was there on the Fourth of July. For nineteenth century emigrants, arrival at the rock by the Fourth of July, Independence Day, was essential if they were to be certain to reach their destinations before snow closed mountain passes to the west.

During the era of overland travel, most people who kept journals or diaries included references to Independence Rock. Rufus Sage, who traveled extensively throughout the region and crossed the trail in 1841, writes:

> Independence Rock is a solid and isolated mass of naked granite, situated about three hundred yards from the right bank of the Sweet Water. It covers an area of four or five acres, and rises to a height of nearly three hundred feet. The general shape is oval, with the exception of a slight depression in its summit where a scanty soil supports a few shrubs and a solitary dwarf-pine.
>
> It derives its name from a party of Americans on their way to Oregon . . . who celebrated the fourth of July at

this place,—they being the first company of whites that ever made the journey from the States, via South Pass.

The surface is covered with the names of travellers, traders, trappers, and emigrants, engraven upon it in almost every practicable part, for the distance of many feet above its base,—but most prominent among them all is the word "Independence," inscribed by the patriotic band who first christened this lonely monument of nature in honor of Liberty's birthday (Sage 1857, n.p.).

This granite outcrop is the largest natural trail register and is now operated as a Wyoming State Park midway between Rawlins and Casper on Route 220.

Inyan Kara Mountain 🌲 🛶 🏴
Crook County

Lieutenant Colonel George Armstrong Custer camped near this mountain in 1874 as he led a scientific and exploring expedition through the Black Hills that are now in both Wyoming and South Dakota. On this trip, Custer's party discovered the gold that led to the subsequent Black Hills Gold Rush. While camped near Inyan Kara, Custer climbed the peak, carving "74 Custer" on a rock at its peak. The peak is located fourteen miles south of Sundance east of Wyoming Highway 585.

Jenney Stockade 🏛 🛶 🚃
Weston County

Professor Walter P. Jenney, a geologist with the Columbia School of Mines in New York, led a scientific party into the Black Hills in 1875 to determine whether the gold reported by Lieutenant Colonel George Armstrong Custer's expedition of the previous year was in substantial quantities or limited amounts. The 1875 Black Hills Expedition (sometimes called the Black Hills Scientific Party) organized at Fort Laramie and traveled north over a route that would eventually become the Cheyenne to Black Hills (Deadwood) stage route (and is now essentially U. S. 85). Jenney stopped at the east fork of Beaver Creek and began construction of a wooden stockade,

which took his name and served the stage road. The Jenney
Stockade became a stage station in 1877.

Although the Black Hills had been set aside for the Lakota
Indians under treaty provisions of 1868, as a result of the gold discoveries made by Custer's 1874 expedition, miners had started moving into the region. When he built the stockade, Jenney estimated
some eight hundred white people were already in the area (Kime
1996). The original Jenney Stockade has been moved to Newcastle
where it is a part of the Anna Miller Museum.

Jerry's Place
Carbon County

Located at the confluence of Muddy Creek and the Little Snake
River, this station served the Rawlins to Baggs and the Baggs to
Wamsutter stage and freight roads and was also known as the
Muddy Bridge Station. It was named for Jerry, a madam who had a
brothel at the station.

Johnson County Invasion/War
Johnson County

On April 5, 1892, a train rolled into Casper from Cheyenne. When
it stopped, gun-toting men from Wyoming, Texas, and Idaho climbed
down from it. The train, known as "The Invasion Special," had three
stockcars filled with horses, a car filled with supplies, a flat car holding three Studebaker wagons, and a passenger car where the gunmen
had ridden. After organizing their gear, the men rode north toward
Buffalo to set in motion an event known as the Johnson County
Invasion and sometimes called the Johnson County War.

The event was precipitated by a period of livestock rustling and
homesteader encroachment onto open range that Wyoming's prominent cattlemen considered their own, even though they didn't hold
title to it. Various incidents involving cattlemen and homesteaders or
rustlers had occurred during the three years leading up to the invasion, including the lynching of Ellen "Cattle Kate" Watson and Jim
Averill (*see* Cattle Kate & James Averill Lynch Site), and the deaths
of rustlers in the Powder River Basin. Finally the cattlemen decided
to put a stop to livestock theft, so they hired the gunmen from Texas

and Idaho, took their own guns, and headed to Johnson County. They had with them a list of men they intended to force out of the country or kill.

On April 9, 1892, the invaders learned that some of the men on their list were present at the KC Ranch, about forty-five miles south of Buffalo and near the southern edge of the present town of Kaycee. The Regulators, as they became known, surrounded the ranch house even though only four men were inside: Nick Ray, Nate Champion, Ben Jones, and Bill Walker. Having no quarrel with Walker and Jones, the cattlemen allowed the two to leave the ranch house unmolested, but they attacked Champion and Ray. When Ray exited the house shortly after breakfast, the invaders shot him. He fled back into the structure where Champion tended his wounds through the day until his death. Champion knew he was in a tight spot, but he recorded what was happening in a small notebook: "Boys, I feel pretty lonesome just now. I wish there was someone here with me so we could watch all sides at once. They may fool around until I get a good shot before they leave" (Champion 1892).

The invaders did not fool around and they did not leave. Late that afternoon Jack Flagg, a friend of Champion, and Flagg's stepson, Alonza Taylor, drove Flagg's wagon past the ranch house. Seeing the invaders surrounding the structure, Flagg immediately realized what was happening and he fled toward Buffalo. It was good he did so as his name was on the dead list the invading force carried. Shortly after Flagg went by, the invaders made a final assault on the ranch house. Champion recorded the scene in a makeshift journal:

> Well, they have just got through shelling the house again like hail. I heard them splitting wood. I guess they are going to fire the house tonight. I think I will make a break when night comes, if alive.

> Shooting again. I think they will fire the house this time.

> It's not night yet. The house is all fired. Goodbye, boys, if I never see you again.

Unable to flush him from the house, the invaders filled a wagon with hay and set it on fire before pushing it into the ranch cabin.

When Champion emerged from the burning structure, they peppered him with bullets. With the invaders at the time was *Chicago Herald* reporter Sam Clover, who was given Champion's small notebook after it was taken from his body by Major Frank Wolcott, one of the well-known Wyoming cattlemen who helped organize the invasion. The journal was initially published in the *Cheyenne Daily Leader* on April 14, 1892, and two days later it was published in the *Chicago Herald.*

After killing Champion, the Regulators mounted their horses and took their wagons to continue north toward Buffalo where they expected to find the rest of the men on their dead list. They reached a point about fourteen miles south of Buffalo when they met a force of men who had organized upon learning from Jack Flagg that an invasion was underway. In the face of such heated opposition, the invading force retreated to the TA Ranch, taking refuge in barns and buildings by Sunday evening, April 10. Soon they were surrounded and besieged just as Ray and Champion had been.

Throughout the day of April 11, the invaders remained at the TA. That night one man or perhaps two men snuck through the lines and sent a message to Wyoming Governor Amos Barber, seeking help. The governor was already aware of the the invasion plan, as were the state's other highest leaders. The governor responded by contacting Wyoming Senators Francis E. Warren and Joseph M. Carey, who themselves went to see President Benjamin Harrison asking for troops to be deployed from Fort McKinney. Harrison gave the order to his Secretary of War that eventually went down the chain of commend to Fort McKinney's Colonel Van Horn, and on the morning of Wednesday, April 12, the colonel and 106 troops from Company VI rode to the TA Ranch to take custody of the Regulators (O'Neal 2004).

Initially taken to Buffalo, the Regulators were not released to Johnson County authorities because Colonel Van Horn feared if he did so a lynch mob would hang the cattlemen and their hired gun force: the general public had made it clear they did not support the actions of the cattlemen who had ridden north from Casper. Instead authorities took the invaders to Cheyenne and jailed them; later they were released on their own recognizance. Charges were filed and a trial commenced. Efforts to seat a jury failed, and on January 18, 1893, officials dropped all charges. None of the invaders ever faced prosecution.

Jumbo Station
Carbon County
This station on the Rawlins to Baggs stage and freight road was located north of Baggs.

Junction House
Goshen County
This is another name for the Cold Springs Station. (*See* Pony Express Trail.)

La Prairie de la Messe
Sublette County
Father Pierre De Smet, a Jesuit Priest originally from Belgium, celebrated the first Roman Catholic Mass in what is now Wyoming at a mountain man rendezvous in 1840 near the present town of Daniel. An altar of green boughs was built for the mass De Smet led in both French and English. Mountain men and Indians were in attendance at the site overlooking the confluence of Horse Creek with the Green River. A cross dedicated to the mass has now been placed overlooking the area where De Smet gathered willing participants for his mass. To reach the site, take Road 188, or DeSmet Road, to the west about five miles south of Daniel Junction.

LaBonte Station
Converse County
Stagecoaches and the Pony Express used the LaBonte Station, which was located on LaBonte Creek about ten miles south of present Douglas. The station is apparently named for a hunter whose Indian wives were killed by other hostile Indians in the area.

William Henry Jackson traveled through the area in 1866, and in his writings, he mentions the "ruins of Fort La Bonte," which had apparently been burned that year (1940, 125). The station had a stockade about 150 feet square made of cottonwood logs placed side

Lake Creek Stage Station served travelers until the early 1900s. (*Courtesy Grand Encampment Museum*)

by side and upright. Those log walls also served as exterior walls for the station's buildings. The kitchen was in the northwest corner, with lodging quarters on the south side. The west wall had a gate in the center while stables lined the east wall. LaBonte Station, which also served as a telegraph station, was renamed Camp Marshall in 1865 (Dilts 1953).

LaClede Station
Sweetwater County
This was a station, or possibly later a ranch, on the Overland Trail located approximately a mile and a half downstream from Fort LaClede on Bitter Creek southwest of Wamsutter. The building was constructed from sandstone and limestone. (*See* Overland Trail.)

Lake Creek Stage Station
Carbon County
Situated about two miles north of present Saratoga on the banks of Lake Creek just off Wyoming Highway 130, this stage station served travelers on the various stage lines running between Grand

This Lake Creek Stage Company receipt dates from 1904. (*Courtesy Grand Encampment Museum*)

Encampment, Warm Springs/Saratoga, and Walcott or Fort Fred Steele from the late 1870s until the early 1900s.

Though many stage lines served the area, including the Fort Steele and Saratoga Stage Line and the Grand Encampment Stage Line, the one Charles M. Scribner operated, first called the Short Line Stage Company and later known as the Scribner Stage Line, is the best known and was the longest lasting. Scribner lived at Lake Creek Stage Station with his family in an L-shaped, multiple room log cabin large enough to serve both travelers and his family. The Scribner line became known for one special stagecoach team, the White Six: horses named White Wing, Dan, Coyote, Curly, Haggarty, and Slim. Scribner's best-known driver, Charley Wilcox, came to the area from Nebraska in 1883 to work on the L7 Ranch owned by Alexander Swan. In a 1903 article, the *Saratoga Sun* reports that Scribner:

> purchased the stages, barns, good-will, etc., of George Nuzum and the latter retired from the stage business, leaving the field to Mr. Scribner. For the past year two lines have

operated between the railroad and Encampment, and there has been cutting of prices on passenger and express rates right and left, a process which left neither line with a profit after expenses were paid. There is room for one good stage line here, such as Mr. Scribner has always run, and there is not room for more (Scribner Buys Nuzum Out 1903, 1).

One two-room portion of the original Lake Creek Stage Station has been moved to the Grand Encampment Museum, and it is open to the public. It includes many items from the Scribner family collection.

Lander Road

Sublette County

In 1857 Brigadier General Frederick W. Lander supervised construction of the first government engineered and financed road in Wyoming. General Lander and half a dozen engineers left South Pass on July 15, 1857, as they began laying out the route of what became the Lander Road.

That initial party surveyed several routes to the north and west, including sixteen different mountain passes. Eventually Lander's route crossed along the Sandy Creek and Green River to Thompson Pass, following a route that basically lies parallel to Wyoming Highway 351 between Big Sandy and Marbleton and then follows north of Wyoming Highway 350 from Marbleton west over the Salt Range and into Star Valley before leaving Wyoming near Afton.

Road construction began June 14, 1858, by a combined force of army engineers, lumbermen, Maine bridge builders, and Mormon laborers who established fifteen miles of road on some days, in part because the terrain was fairly level and covered only with sagebrush or greasewood. The road opened for use by Oregon-bound emigrants in 1859 and remained in use until 1912.

The route was known as the Pacific Wagon Road, and the government also designated it as the Fort Kearney [sic]–South Pass–City of Rocks–Honey Lake Road, so named for the major points along its route (Wight 1993, i).

LaPrele Station 🚏
Converse County
Stage lines and the Pony Express used this station at the trail crossing of LaPrele Creek about ten miles west of present Douglas. It also served as a telegraph station. The site had four log cabins in addition to the station itself, a root cellar, and a well. The station was about a quarter of a mile southeast of where the Rock Creek–Fort Fetterman Road crossed the Oregon Trail.

Nearby are two graves. One holds six-year-old Joel Hembree, who fell from the wagon on which he traveled with the first large party of Oregon Trail emigrants in 1843. He was run over by the wagon and killed on July 18, 1843, and is the first casualty of the "great migration" (*see also* Joel Hembree Grave). The other grave holds the remains of Private Ralston Baker, Company E, Eleventh Ohio Cavalry, who died May 1, 1867 (Edwards 1953, as reported in Carley 1956). In his journal on July 20, 1843, Oregon-bound emigrant James W. Nesmith writes:

> At noon came up to a fresh grave with stones piled over it, and a note tied on a stick, informing us that it was the grave of Joel J. Hembree, aged six years, who was killed by a wagon running over its body. At the head of the grave stood a stone containing the name of the child, the first death on the expedition. The grave is on the left hand side of the trail close to Squaw Butte Creek [LaPrele Creek].

Laramie, Laramie Peak, Laramie Plains, Laramie Range, Laramie River 🌲
Albany, Laramie, Platte, and Goshen Counties
The various landmarks in southeastern Wyoming known as Laramie all take their name from trapper Jacques la Ramee.

Lightning Creek, Battle of 🏴 ⛺
Niobrara County
Certainly one of the final Indian battles in Wyoming, the fight at Lightning Creek in 1903 took place midway between Lance Creek and Bill, east of Wyoming Highway 59.

Approximately twenty-five reservation Lakota Indians were en route back to South Dakota after a hunting trip to Montana when they met a posse led by Newcastle Sheriff W. H. "Billy" Miller. Not only had the Indians left the reservation without permission, they also reportedly broke newly approved game laws. At any rate, in the fight that occurred between the Indians and the posse, Sheriff Miller was killed along with Jackie Mills and Deputy Louis Falkenburg. Several of the Indians also died in the incident before the others, including He Dog and Eagle Feather (known also as Charlie Smith), fled. In the wake of the fighting, Lee Mathews took charge of the posse pursuing the Indians until they finally surrendered near Hat Creek Station. Both He Dog and Eagle Feather eventually faced charges, but in a court hearing held in Douglas, no proof was presented that clearly outlined the events of the October 30, 1903, fight. The court acquitted the Indians.

Little Bear Stage Station
Laramie County

Isaac Bard claimed a 160-acre homestead on Little Bear Creek and developed a road ranch that served travelers on the Cheyenne to Black Hills stage route. He notes in his diary on April 28, 1876, "I will now try keeping a public house if the Lord is willing and the Indians let me alone" (Wyoming Recreation Commission 1988, 147). He had some difficulty with thieves, but his ranch in 1877 became a stage station stop known as the Little Bear Station for the Cheyenne–Black Hills stage route. This station is on private land north of Cheyenne.

Little Box Elder, Indian attack
Converse County

Josiah Kelley, his wife, Fanny Wiggins Kelly, and their adopted daughter, Mary, were traveling west over the Oregon–California Trail in the summer of 1864 when Lakotas attacked their wagons near Little Box Elder Creek. With the Kelly family were several other travelers, including Gardner Wakefield, Mr. Larimer, his wife, Sarah, and their eight-year-old son, a Methodist minister known as Mr. Sharp, another man remembered as Mr. Taylor, and two Black servants, Frank and Andy. When the small party met a much larger group of Lakotas on July 12 near Little Box Elder Creek, the emigrants believed the Indians only wanted food, but as the men began to get supplies to give to the Indians, the situation turned hostile.

Before the initial shooting subsided, Wakefield had been mortally wounded, and Sharp, Taylor, and Frank were all dead. The Indians looted the contents of the wagons then took Sarah Larimer and her son as well as Fanny and Mary Kelly with them when they left the scene. The surviving men had hidden in the area and were unable to protect the women and children.

Mrs. Larimer and her son escaped the Indians two days later, finding their way back to the trail. Fannie Kelly also helped Mary evade the Indians, telling her to follow their tracks back to the location where the attack had occurred. The girl did so and soldiers spotted her there, but seeing Indians in the area, the soldiers did not ride to the girl and instead returned to Deer Creek Station, where they found Kelly. Upon hearing reports of the young girl, he persuaded soldiers to go to the area. When they arrived they found Mary dead, shot with several arrows. Meanwhile, the Indians held Fannie for five months until eventually releasing her at Fort Sully in present North Dakota (Morrison 1971).

Little Laramie Station 🚉
Albany County

This Overland Trail station located at the confluence of the Little Laramie River and Brown's Creek had corrals, a blacksmith shop, and a station house built of logs by Philip Mandel, a native of Alsace, France. He had been with the U. S. Army during the 1857 Mormon, or Utah, War and later made his way to the Little Laramie, where he filed a homestead claim in 1864, the first in the area. While in the army, Mandel had met Ben Holladay, who operated the Overland Stage Company through this area beginning in 1862, which no doubt inspired Mandel to stake his claim there. He was known to harvest native grass for feed to sell to Fort Sanders and to provide travelers with a meal or "free plots for burial" (Carley 1961a, 88).

Indians attacked nine members of the First Colorado Cavalry Regiment on Seven Mile Creek west of the Little Laramie Station in August 1862. The troops were escorting two government supply wagons at the time. One private was killed in the incident (Interview with E. N. Lewis 1865).

Little Muddy Station 🚂
Natrona County
This is another name for the Pony Express station at Glenrock (*see entry*).

Little Sandy Station 🚂
Sweetwater County
This was a Pony Express relay station in 1860 and 1861 located on Little Sandy Creek east of Farson. The site is now on public land, and clear depressions in the hillside near the creek indicate the location of the station buildings. (*See* Pony Express Trail.)

Little Snake River, Indian attack 🛶 Å
Carbon County
Trapper Henry Fraeb liked the country of the Little Snake River, and he was there in 1841 when mountain man Jim Bridger became concerned because Fraeb had not reported in as expected at a trading post the two men had opened in southwest Wyoming. Mountain man Jim Baker told Bridger he would go to the Little Snake country to find out what had delayed Fraeb and his companions. Baker found the trappers near the head of the river, and just a week later a combined party of Arapaho, Lakota, and Cheyenne Indians located them as well. On August 21, 1841, the Indians attacked the trapper group at a site that is now private ranch land straddling the present Wyoming-Colorado border. Of this event, Baker writes:

> Shortly after I came out here the second time we were camped on the very creek where I live now—Snake River we called it then—and there we had a lively fight with a party of about 500 Sioux, Cheyenne and Arapahoes. The Arapahoes didn't do much fighting, but they urged the others on. There were twenty-three in our party, and I can give you the names of every one of them. Old Frappe [Fraeb] was in command. The Indians made about forty charges on us,

coming up to within ten or fifteen paces of us every time. Their object was to draw our fire, but old Frappe kept shouting 'Don't shoot till you're sure. One at a time.' And so some of us kept loaded all the time. We made breastworks of our horses and hid behind stumps. Old Frappe was killed, and he was the ugliest looking dead man I ever saw, and I have seen a good many. His face was all covered with blood, and he had rotten front teeth and a horrible grin. When he was killed he never fell, but sat braced up against a stump, a sight to behold. Well, when the fight was over there were about a hundred dead Injuns. There were three of our party killed (Hafen 1930, 97–101).

The Indian party probably numbered nowhere near five hundred; likely the trappers killed far fewer than one hundred Indians. At least four, or possibly as many as eight, trappers died. Several sites get their name from this incident, including Squaw Mountain, Battle Creek, Battle Mountain, and Battle Lake, all accessible by driving Wyoming Highway 70 between Savery and Encampment.

Lombard Ferry 🚌
Sweetwater County
This ferry over the Green River served traffic at a site near the mouth of the Big Sandy River on the present Seedskadee National Wildlife Area. The ferry was an important crossing site because fording the Green River was difficult in even the best of circumstances—early in spring and late in summer when water flows were reduced—and very dangerous or impossible during the high water of early summer. Mormons put in the first ferry in the area in 1847, and other ferries followed by 1849, all commercial ventures, charging from three to four dollars for each wagon to cross.

Lone Tree Station 🚌
Sweetwater County
A swing station, where stagecoaches changed teams, on the Overland Trail west of Green River, this site is now on private land. (*See* Overland Trail.)

Mad River 🌲
Teton and Sublette Counties

Trappers called the Snake River in northwest Wyoming the Mad River, according to Washington Irving in his book *Astoria*, because it was both fast and turbulent. The Astorian Party of Pierre Dorion, Jr., led by John Hoback, Jacob Reznor, and Edward Robinson, made its way down the river in 1811, and Irving describes their pleasure at returning to their preferred mode of travel:

> The Canadian voyageurs rejoiced at the idea of once more launching themselves upon their favorite element, of ex-changing their horses for canoes, and of gliding down the bosoms of rivers, instead of scrambling over the backs of mountains (1839, 223).

Martin's Cove 🎏 🛒
Natrona County

In 1856 five companies of Mormons from England and Scandinavia migrated toward Deseret [Utah] under a new travel plan that had the travelers haul their goods by using handcarts. Such companies had a small number of wagons attached to them to haul supplies and carry any travelers who were ill or injured. Captain Edward Martin led the Fifth Handcart Company, comprising 856 travelers, which left late in the season. The party reached the North Platte River, crossing near what is now Casper in mid-October. Snow was already hitting them in the face. As the weather turned colder and winter storms began sweeping across the region, the people ran out of food. Many of them became ill and subsequently died after crossing the icy North Platte River. Ahead of the Martin Company, James Grey Willie led the 764 members of the Fourth Handcart Company, and though they were farther west along the trail, they, too, were without adequate food and clothing.

The first three companies totaling 1,019 people had already reached Great Salt Lake City, and missionaries for the Mormon Church were there as well. They told Mormon Leader Brigham Young that hundreds of Saints were still out on the trail and in desperate need of assistance. Young immediately organized rescue parties that set out in early October from Great Salt Lake City headed toward the Willie and Martin parties. The rescuers had teams and wagons filled with provisions. As Young had ordered, the relief wagons were pulled by mules, which traveled more quickly than oxen.

The Martin party stopped for days after crossing the North Platte in an area likely near Red Buttes west of present Casper and eventually traveled on west to Horse Creek. The Willie party was farther west along the Sweetwater River when the first rescuers found both parties. In both cases, rescuers told the handcart companies they had to keep moving west because so many people needed help and not enough rescue wagons were oncoming to haul everyone.

The Willie Company continued west and were met by the second group of rescuers just east of South Pass. The Martin Company also resumed travel, eventually making its way to near Devil's Gate where some people took refuge in the deteriorating buildings of Seminoe's Fort (*see entry*). But when winter storms continued, the Martin Company members picked up their handcarts once again, waded the freezing waters of the Sweetwater River, and took refuge in a naturally sheltered area that subsequently became known as Martin's Cove.

In spite of the rescue efforts, from 135 to 156 members of the Martin Company died, many of them in the area of Martin's Cove, and seventy members of the Willie Company died.

As a result of the difficulties, the land around Martin's Cove is considered sacred ground by Mormon people, as is the region near Rock Creek, farther west, where the Willie party lost fifteen members in a two-day span just as rescuers located that party. Martin's Cove is federal land now leased to the Church of Jesus Christ of Latter-day Saints, while the church manages the Rock Creek site. Both sites are open to the general public. Martin's Cove is near the Sun Ranch, also called the Handcart Ranch, midway between Casper and Rawlins and adjacent to Wyoming Highway 220. The Rock Creek site is accessible on Bureau of Land Management and Fremont County roads that pass through Atlantic City. (*See also* Horse Creek Station.)

In spite of the disaster affecting the Willie and Martin Companies, handcart travel continued. According to figures LeRoy and

Ann Hafen compiled in *Handcarts to Zion* (1960), in 1857 an additional 1,321 people immigrated to Great Salt Lake City with handcart companies. Another 725 crossed in 1859, and two companies comprising 1,324 people pulled and pushed handcarts across the trail in 1860.

Maynadier Expedition ⥤
Powder River, Wind River, and Big Horn Basins

Lieutenant H. E. Maynadier led the first government exploration of the Wind River Canyon and Big Horn Basin in 1860. In 1859, Maynardier traveled with Captain W. F. Raynolds, crossing through present western South Dakota and eastern Montana before dividing the party near the confluence of the Little Big Horn River with the Yellowstone River. Both then traveled south, with Raynolds, guided by Jim Bridger, moving west and then south along the eastern foothills of the Big Horn Mountains. Maynardier, meanwhile, turned due south and followed Clear Creek downstream to its confluence with Crazy Woman Creek, which he then followed upstream, before rejoining Raynolds and traveling south to winter near the North Platte River at the Upper Platte River Indian Agency near present-day Glenrock.

The combined parties spent the winter drafting maps and making plans for explorations the following summer. The next year in 1860 Maynadier traveled along the Oregon Trail past Independence Rock and then up the Sweetwater River before he turned north into the Wind River Basin, and then followed the Big Horn River into the Big Horn Basin. His party located gold in the Big Horn Basin but had difficulty getting wagons into the area and later lost mules and supplies in the Stinking Water (Shoshone) River. Much of Maynadier's route through the Big Horn Basin was along what would become the Bridger Trail a few short years later (*see entry*).

Bridger was not with Maynadier and instead guided Raynolds across western Wyoming, traveling just west of what would become Yellowstone National Park and then north into present Montana. Raynolds and Maynadier's parties reconnoitered for a time in western Montana before taking separate routes across that region on their east-bound journeys.

The surveys of Raynolds and Maynadier resulted in new maps of much of Wyoming. In particular, Maynardier's explorations into the Big Horn Basin provided new detail about that region's resources. The outbreak of the Civil War, however, delayed the final reports, which were not complete until 1868. The maps they made, particularly of the Powder River Basin, became an important resource for the frontier army during the Indian wars in that region in 1876 (Brown 1969). Maynadier would later command Fort Laramie (*see entry*).

Medicine Bow Overland Trail Station
Carbon County

Located beside the Medicine Bow River not far from the present town of Elk Mountain, this Overland Trail station is now on private land. Edward Ordway traveled the trail in 1867, writing:

> The stage company had only one building, a long log stable arranged in the usual way, stalls on each side for horses and spaces for hay and grain, with an alley running from front to back through the middle and a large room partitioned off in the southwest corner for the stocktenders to live in, with a trap door in the floor leading into a tunnel which ran under the road into a small fort opposite the alley way through the stable. There was a lot of timber and brush on both sides of the river which made it easy for the Indians to watch an opportunity to slip into the back end of the stable and get away with the horses (Ordway 1929, 180).

Medicine Bow Union Pacific Station
Carbon County

This station on the Union Pacific Railroad served as an important freight point for civilian and military supplies after 1868. Among supplies shipped through Medicine Bow Station for use by troops involved in the Powder River Expedition in the fall of 1876 were cavalry jackets, rubber blankets, ponchos, woolen mittens, blankets, and rubber overshoes (Greene 2003). The station evolved into the town of Medicine Bow, made famous by Owen Wister in his novel *The Virginian*.

Medicine Wheel 🚏 ⩓
Big Horn County

One of the most sacred sites for American Indians sits high atop the Big Horn Mountains in northern Wyoming. The Medicine Wheel is an arrangement of rocks in a pattern that resembles a wagon wheel. Also in the area are other rock markers, including stone cairns and rock arrows. Prayer bundles have been left on trees, the fence around the Medicine Wheel, and at other locations nearby. Today the site is a National Historic Landmark administered by the U. S. Forest Service; yet, it remains culturally important for many tribes. The Medicine Wheel is about an hour drive east of Lovell at an elevation of nearly 10,000 feet.

Menor's Ferry 🚃
Teton County, Grand Teton National Park

Early settler William Menor constructed a ferry over the Snake River in 1892, placing it west of Blacktail Butte and near the present community of Moose and the headquarters of Grand Teton National Park. The ferry soon became an important economic center for the area, and Menor also operated a small store. He sold the ferry in 1918 to Maude Noble. In 1927, officials met in Noble's home to discuss the first legislation that set aside the Grand Teton mountain range as Grand Teton National Park; the park was subsequently expanded in 1943. Some of Menor's ranch buildings and his ferry remain. The ferry has been restored as a working ferry. Reach it by entering Grand Teton National Park at Moose and then turning right into a parking lot at the Chapel of the Transfiguration.

Midway/Charles Bird Stage Stop 🚃
Lincoln County

This station served the Opal Wagon Road that opened in 1882, serving traffic between Opal and communities to the north, including Cora and Pinedale. The station, known both as Midway and as the Charles Bird Stage Stop, was improved in 1889 with a twelve-room house that remained at the site until it burned in 1934. It is on private land.

Military Telegraph Lines 📧

In 1861 the first transcontinental telegraph line, sometimes called the Creighton Telegraph, was built by civilian contractors and followed the Oregon Trail route across Wyoming. Its completion led to the demise of the Pony Express. A second telegraph line was constructed along the Overland Trail route in 1865 and 1866. The military also constructed several telegraph lines linking forts and Indian agencies with stations along the Union Pacific right-of-way. Other telegraph lines were in place along the Bozeman Trail and along the route of the Rawlins to Fort Washakie Road.

Millersville Station 🚃
Sweetwater County

This site served as a Pony Express relay station in 1860 and 1861. It was located east of Fort Bridger. (*See* Pony Express Trail.)

Mormon Ferry 🚃
Natrona County

In 1847 members of the Church of Jesus Christ of Latter-day Saints (the Mormons) led by Brigham Young pushed west from Winter Quarters (Florence, Nebraska) to a new homeland they established in the Great Salt Lake Valley. When the travelers reached the area that is present Casper, they needed to cross the North Platte River. Knowing hundreds of families would follow them, Young's Pioneer Party established a ferry over the river at a site near present Fort Caspar. The ferry operated through 1851. It was no longer needed after 1852 because by then the overland travelers could use the Richard/Reshaw Bridge (*see entry*).

Mormon Mail Service

Hiram Kimball obtained a contract from the U. S. government in 1856 to carry mail from Fort Laramie to Salt Lake City. Kimball established stage stations at Horseshoe, LaBonte, Deer Creek, Sweetwater (Independence Rock), Devil's Gate, and Fort Bridger to conduct the Morman Mail Service as it was known. Other stations were located between Devil's Gate and Fort Bridger, likely near South Pass and Big Sandy.

The Mormon Trail is still visible at this location east of Independence Rock. (*Candy Moulton*)

Mormon Trail
Goshen, Platte, Converse, Natrona, Carbon, Fremont, Sweetwater, and Uinta Counties

In 1846, Mormons from Nauvoo, Illinois, migrated west to avoid religious persecution. They spent the winter of 1846–1847 in a camp they called Winter Quarters that is now in the city of Florence, Nebraska.

In 1847 a Pioneer Party led by Brigham Young forged a route west that followed the Platte River through present Nebraska and then the North Platte River into present Wyoming. The route the Mormons took to the Great Salt Lake Valley, where they established a new city and made homes for themselves, generally followed the north bank of the North Platte River to what is now Casper. From there the route was roughly the same as the Oregon Trail, following the Sweetwater River to South Pass and then continuing west to near Farson and the Green River before turning south to Fort Bridger.

Knowing that many other Mormon families would follow them, the first travelers over the Mormon Trail made improvements to the road. They established ferries at river crossings on the North Platte and Green Rivers. Later they established road ranches or stations, where they could raise or stockpile supplies for travelers. Much of the travel over the Mormon Trail was a two-way operation with wagon trains organized in Deseret (as they called Utah) in the spring moving east over the trail to meet immigrants who had come from England, Scotland, and Scandinavia and provide transportation for them to travel to Great Salt Lake City. Those wagon trains were known as the Down-and-Back Trains.

Used primarily by wagon train travelers, the Mormon Trail became a route for handcart pioneers from 1856 until 1860 when the Church of Jesus Christ of Latter-day Saints President Brigham Young mandated that immigrants should place their belongings in two-wheeled carts and push or pull them west. The handcart travel would be less expensive and, therefore, would enable more converts to the Mormon Church to travel to Utah. Young also believed the immigrants could travel more quickly by handcart than by wagon train. Most of the handcart emigrants were foreigners who had converted to the LDS Church years before they immigrated to America. Generally poor, most traveled under the provisions of the church's Perpetual Emigration Fund (P. E. F.), which was devised by church hierarchy to pay the expenses of those who had little money to come to America. The handcart pioneers traveled by ship to Boston or New York, then by train to Iowa City where they obtained their handcarts. Around 3,000 people immigrated to Deseret/Utah by means of handcarts. (*See also* Martin's Cove.)

Mouseau's Road Ranch 🚜
Platte County
M. A. Mouseau built a road ranch near Twin Springs (or Red Springs) about five miles south of present Glendo to serve emigrant traffic. The ranch, date of origin unknown, sold liquor and supplies before it was destroyed in 1868 during the Battle of Horseshoe Creek.

Muddy Bridge Station 🚚
Carbon County
This station on the Rawlins to Baggs and Baggs to Wamsutter stage and freight roads was also known as Jerry's Place, named for the woman who had a brothel at the station.

Muddy Creek Massacre 🚚 🏴 ⚔
Carbon County
Cheyenne and Lakota Indians attacked an emigrant wagon train between Bridger's Pass and Sulphur Springs along Muddy Creek in August 1863. As there had been escalating difficulties with Indians along the route of the Overland Trail after 1862, the wagon train had a military escort, but when the wagon train stopped at Muddy Creek to fill water barrels, the Indians attacked. Some of the soldiers counterattacked, but when they were away from the train, they were surrounded by Indians and unable to get back to the emigrants. The sound of the battle carried to troops at Sulphur Springs where Major R. A. Morse with troops from Companies A, C, and D, First Kansas Volunteer Cavalry, organized and went to the aid of the emigrants. Upon arrival of the soldiers, the Indians retreated. In the incident, according to an account day book Major Morse kept, twenty-nine men, women, and children were killed, seventeen others were seriously injured, and ten had minor injures. He estimated that ninety Indians were hurt or killed in the fight, though that figure is probably inflated (Erb et al. 1989).

Muddy Creek Station 🚚
Uinta County
This was a Pony Express relay station from 1860 to 1861. (*See* Pony Express Trail.)

Name Rock 🌲 🚚
Uinta County
Located near Millersville, this rock has an 1856 inscription of Mormon prophet Brigham Young's name, though he is not known to have been in the area at that time, making it unlikely that he carved his own name.

Names Hill 🏛 🌲 🛻
Sublette County

Emigrants traveling to California over the Sublette Cutoff carved their names in the sandstone cliff above the Green River that has since been called Names Hill. A ferry across the Green River started operating in 1847. The ferry was located midway between Names Hill and the regular fording place on the Green River about five miles south of LaBarge and west of U. S. 189.

Nez Perce Trail ⛺
Yellowstone National Park

When the Nez Perce Indians left the Wallowa Valley in 1877 and turned to flight rather than settling on the reservation at Lapwai in Idaho, they traveled through present northern Idaho and Montana before turning southeast and crossing into Yellowstone National Park. The Indians were pursued by U. S. Army troops commanded by General Oliver O. Howard, who intended to return them to the reservation. They had various battles in Idaho and western Montana before reaching the Henry's Lake area of Idaho. From there the Indians crossed Targhee Pass and followed the Madison River into Yellowstone National Park. They then moved east through Yellowstone, traveling south of Firehole Canyon, crossing the present Grand Loop Road along a small stream that has since become known as Nez Perce Creek. Then they used Mary's Trail. By this time they had taken as hostages nine Montana tourists who were vacationing in Yellowstone.

The Nez Perce route then continued east to near Mud Volcano where the Indians crossed the Yellowstone River before following the Pelican Valley north. In that area they released the last of their hostages, though some of them had escaped and one, George Cowan, was injured and left for dead (though he wasn't) in an earlier incident. From the northern end of the Pelican Valley, the route of the Nez Perces is not certain. Possibly they followed Timothy Creek and Miller Creek before passing out of the park and eventually traveling down the Clark's Fork of the Yellowstone to the north into Montana Territory.

Some of the Nez Perce warriors continued farther north from Pelican Creek to near Mammoth Hot Springs before turning east across Baronett's Bridge, which they attempted to burn and destroy. Then they followed the East Fork of the Yellowstone River or the Lamar River to cross out of the park somewhere in the northeast corner and join their compatriots.

All the Nez Perces journeyed through the Sunlight Basin and followed the Clark's Fork River to elude soldiers.

On September 16, 1877, in the area of present Dead Indian Campground, Frank Parker, who was scouting and reporting on the incident with the army, writes:

> On the 10th we came to a hostile camp which had just been abandoned, at the base of the last mountain necessary to climb before reaching the buffalo plains at Heart Mountain (1895, as quoted in Wilfong 1990, 264).

That same day, S. G. Fisher, who was traveling with Howard's command, notes that the Indians had driven their horses across the area below Dead Indian Pass to disguise their trail, but the scouts scattered, looking for evidence of the Nez Perce Route. "I final[l]y stumbled on it," Fisher writes. He continues:

> Instead of going out of the bason [sic] on the open plain, they had turned North, passing along the steep side of the Mountain through the timber for several miles. . . . The trail led us through a rough canyon very narrow in places (1877, as quoted in Wilfong 1990, 265).

The Nez Perces had avoided troops by traveling the Clark's Fork country and eventually following the narrow canyon. Howard describes the canyon as:

> . . . not more than twenty feet across from high wall to high wall. And one may imagine the scene of cavalry, infantry, and pack-mules crowding through it and admire the quick wit of an Indian who had the hardihood to try the experiment and break the almost impassable roadway (1881, n.p.).

Once traveling north again, the Nez Perces, still pursued by Howard, continued across Montana Territory toward Canada, where they hoped to find refuge with Sitting Bull, who had taken some of his people there after the battle at the Little Bighorn in 1876. The Nez Perce flight ended at the Bear's Paw in northern Montana just forty miles from the Canadian sanctuary they sought. There the Indians were surrounded by U. S. military troops commanded by Colonel Nelson Miles, who had approached from the southeast. Troops with Miles captured the Indian horse herd, making further flight impossible for most of the Indians, though a few continued to Canada. After a five-day battle and siege, Nez Perce Chief Joseph finally surrendered. At that time he made a speech that has since become famous as he told Miles and Howard, "From where the sun now stands, I will fight no more" (Moulton 2006, 190).[4]

Nine Mile Station
Goshen County
This station on the Pony Express route nine miles west of Fort Laramie also went by the names Sand Point Trading Post, Ward and Guerrier's Trading Post, and Central Star Station.

North Platte Crossing
Carbon County
This Overland Trail and Cherokee Trail station was located on the east side of the North Platte River about nine miles northwest of present Saratoga. Long before the trails were established, Indians had a camp in this same area with around twenty war lodges still in evidence when Howard Stansbury's exploring party passed through the area in 1850.

A ferry operated at the river crossing (*see also* Bennett's Ferry). In October 1862 *Rocky Mountain News* editor Edward Bliss traveled the Overland Trail, writing:

> There is little to attract the attention of the traveler, save the crossing of the North Platte. Preparations are in the making for the establishment of a ferry at this crossing in time for the highwater of the winter and spring months. At present

the ford is an easy and excellent one (1931, 192, as quoted in Alcorn 1984, 23).

Fitzhugh Ludlow reached the area in June 1863. He writes:

We crossed the North Platte by an ingenious contrivance which I here saw for the first time. . . . This is a ferry-boat whose motive power was the current it had to cross. I venture to believe many of my readers as ignorant as I found myself, and endeavor to give some idea of this ingenious contrivance. . . . A stout post, square-hewn from an entire trunk, about eighteen inches in diameter, is driven firmly into each of the opposite bluffs, and between the two, tautened by a windlass, extends a heavy hempen cable, roven [*sic*] through a pair of lignum-vitae double-blocks, of sufficient breadth of eye and depth of groove to run without friction and quite independent of each other, from post to post. . . . The ferry-boat is a rough, strongly built scow, with standing room for (one wagon) or for a four-in-hand team and as many passengers as choose to wedge themselves in between horses and piles of baggage,—a craft apparently of ten or twelve tons burden (1870, 236–237, as quoted in Alcorn 1984, 62).

The ferry moved across the river by using the force of the current itself for power. The charge for a wagon to cross was $5 (Alcorn 1984). At various times the ferry operators were Ed Bennett, Frank Earnest, and Ed Ferguson (Erb et al. 1989).

The crossing was difficult for most travelers as the river usually ran swiftly in this vicinity. A report of one military party comanded by Major Andrew Burt in June 1866 describes one tragic event:

It was not long before a crash came. In a second we saw the boat overturned in the stream; the white wagon top was carried down; mules quickly disappeared and alas, also the three men who were with the wagon. All vanished like a flash. The wagon proved to be one belonging to Company F, and with it was Sergeant St. John and two other good men of the company (Mattes 1960, 65).[5]

Old Bellewood Stage Station and Hotel 🚌
Platte County
This post office and hotel was on Horseshoe Creek south of present
Glendo. It was run by Fred and Bridget McDermott between 1887
and 1892 and was named for their daughter Isabelle. The stage
between Wendover and Fort Fetterman stopped here.

Old Platte Bridge 🌉 🚌
Natrona County
When travelers traveled west over the Oregon, California, and Mormon Trails from 1841 to 1869, their routes in present Wyoming generally all followed the North Platte River, which they crossed in the
area between today's Glenrock and Casper. Several ferries operated,
and bridges also served the trail traffic. Old Platte Bridge was one of
those crossing points, built by Louis Guinard in 1858.

In 1860 Sir Richard Burton followed the trail, writing:

> Our station lay near the upper crossing or second bridge, a
> short distance from the town. It was also built of timber at
> an expense of $40,000, [this figure appears highly inflated]
> about a year ago, by Louis Guenot [Guinard] a Quebec-
> quois, who has passed the last twelve years upon the plains
> (Burton 1862; reprint 1990, 141).

Old Rock Ranch 🚌
Goshen County
Located about three and one-half miles west of present Torrington
and believed to have been a trading post, this site had two buildings—one fifteen by thirty feet made of cedar logs and the other
constructed of a rough masonry.

One Mile Hog Ranch
Converse County
Located a scant mile from Fort Fetterman and some ten miles west
of present Douglas on Wyoming Highway 93, this is probably Wyoming's most notorious hog ranch—and the name does not mean
that pigs were the commodity sold or traded there. This hog ranch,

constructed by Harry Cain, offered women, whiskey, and gambling in a fifty-foot-long log building beginning in the fall of 1882. It was also known as the Fort Fetterman Hog Ranch. Later partners in the operation were Jack Sanders and John D. Lawrence, and then William "Billy" Bacon became a partner. On November 30, 1885, Sanders and Bacon were involved in a shootout, killing each other as a result. The operation closed soon after.

Oregon Trail 〒 ⌐ 🏚

Goshen, Platte, Converse, Natrona, Carbon, Fremont, Sweetwater, Sublette, Uinta, and Lincoln Counties

Wild game and Indians used the first major overland trail long before emigrants took wagons to Oregon Country. The first American expedition to follow the route traveled it in 1812 when Robert Stuart and six companions left Fort Astoria on the Oregon coast in late summer and headed east. With information from Indians, they crossed into present Wyoming by following the Snake River before traveling south along the west side of the Continental Divide. They are credited with discovering the great South Pass that became the later key to Oregon migration, though they crossed the Continental Divide at a location south of the actual South Pass, most likely making their way through either Crooks Gap or possibly Muddy Gap farther to the south.

Once east of the Divide, Stuart and his companions struck the Sweetwater River, no doubt passing near what would become Independence Rock, before taking off cross-country to the North Platte River. They reached the area near the Red Buttes and Bessemer Bend (six miles west of present Casper) in the fall and decided to spend the winter there, in part because of the river and its source of water for both man and animal. The region also had plenty of game for food during a long winter. Stuart and his companions built a cabin and prepared for cold weather, but a party of Indians—probably Arapahos—found their camp, so Stuart abandoned the cabin and continued on down the Platte River, eventually settling in for the winter near the present border between Wyoming and Nebraska east of Torrington.

In the 1820s mountain men began following the route Stuart and his companions had taken, and in 1824 Jedediah Smith, William Sublette, and Tom Fitzpatrick crossed South Pass, essentially rediscovering it. In 1832 explorer Benjamin L. E. Bonneville took the first wagons over the pass. The first white women to cross the trail were Narcissa Whitman and Eliza Spalding, who traveled with a fur brigade and their missionary husbands over the route in 1836 to the mountain rendezvous at the Green River before eventually continuing on to found the Whitman Mission—Waiilatpu—near present Walla Walla, Washington, and the Spalding Mission at Lapwai, Idaho. That passage by white women, who rode horseback on sidesaddles or in wagons, made it clear to people back east that women could follow the trail west successfully. A subsequent migration began with a small wagon party in 1841 followed by a one-thousand wagon caravan in 1843, a year most often considered the beginning of the Oregon Trail. Before trail travel ceased in 1869 with the completion of the transcontinental railroad, more than 400,000 people had traveled across Wyoming over the main route of the Oregon Trail and its many side roads.

It took emigrants about six months to travel from Independence, Missouri, where the Oregon Trail started, to their final destinations, and generally they spent about a month on the trail in what is now Wyoming. Those going to Oregon most often used oxen to pull their wagons. Wagon trains were like mobile communities, with leaders selected at the beginning of the trip, but they were also fluid, and often parties separated so some could travel more quickly or to reach different destinations. Wagon parties included family groups and also individuals who did not previously know each other but who banded together for protection as they often believed there was danger from Indians. In the early years of trail travel, there were no attacks on wagon trains by Indians, and, in fact, the native Americans were often quite helpful, providing information about the route or trading supplies to the emigrants. In the 1860s, on rare occasions, Indians did harass trail travelers, staging some outright attacks in Idaho.

The same basic travel corridor was used beginning in 1847 by Mormons headed to Deseret (as they called Utah) and in 1849 by Argonauts en route to California's gold fields. Although there are variations of the trails in Wyoming, in most areas of central and western Wyoming, the Oregon, California, and Mormon Trails were generally the same. The same trail corridor also became the route of the Pony Express in 1860 and of the transcontinental telegraph line in 1861 (*see* Pony Express Trail and Military Telegraph Lines).

Among the significant trail sites in Wyoming are Register Cliff, Guernsey Ruts, Deer Creek, North Platte Crossing (at Casper) where there were eventually ferries and bridges over the river, Avenue of Rocks or Emigrant Gap, Independence Rock, Devil's Gate, Split Rock, South Pass, Pacific Springs, Parting of the Ways, and Green River (which eventually had ferry service). Two pioneer forts anchored the trail: Fort Laramie in the eastern part of the present state and Fort Bridger in the west (*see individual entries*).

Oregon Trail Ruts �︎ 🚃
Platte County

Often referred to as the Guernsey Ruts or Deep Rut Hill, this signature cut into the sandstone one and one-half miles southeast of Guernsey accessible via Road 109S, may have started as a result of travel over the Oregon Trail, but almost certainly the deep cut was enhanced by military traffic traveling to and from Fort Laramie. This site is now managed by the state of Wyoming, and there is a hiking trail to the ruts.

Overland Mail Service

In early 1862 the Overland Mail Service followed the Oregon–California road across what is now central Wyoming. But as conflict with Indians increased along the route, the military issued orders to change the route to a more southerly location that followed the Cherokee Trail across what is now southern Wyoming (and which became known as the Overland Trail as a result).

A letter from James Craig to General James G. Blunt written at Fort Laramie, July 11, 1862, outlines the issues of the day.

> GENERAL: I am in receipt to-day of a dispatch informing me that the Postmaster-General has ordered the Overland Mail Company to abandon the North Platte and Sweet

Water portion of the route and remove their stages and stock to a route south of this running through the Bridger Pass. As I feel uncertain as to my duty, and as the stages and stock are now being concentrated preparatory to removal, I have thought proper to sent Lieutenant Wilcox, Fourth U. S. Cavalry, to you with this letter. My instructions require me to protect the overland mail along the telegraph line, and the emigration not being mentioned, I have up to this time directed my attention to the safety of all these. My recollection of the act of Congress is that the mail company are not confined to any particular pass or route, but are to run from the Missouri River to a point in California daily, supplying Denver City and Salt Lake City twice a week. On the application of agents I have to-day ordered two small escorts, one of 25, the other of 30, men, to accompany the stages and protect them to the new route, and until I receive your orders I will retain upon the present route the larger portion of the troops to protect the telegraph line and the emigration, at least until the emigration, which consists principally of family trains, has passed through my district. I do this because the Indians evince a disposition to rob the trains and destroy the [telegraph] wires. Indeed I am satisfied that unless the Government is ready to abandon this route both for mails and emigrants an Indian war is inevitable. All the tribes in these mountains, except perhaps one of the Lenox [possibly he meant Shoshone] bands, are in bad humor; charge the Government with bad faith and breaches of promise in failing to send them an agent and presents. They have come in by hundreds from the Upper Missouri, attacked and robbed emigrant trains and mail stations and in one instant last week they robbed a mail station within two hours after a detachment of Colonel [William O.] Collins' troops had passed, and carried the herdsman away with them to prevent him from notifying the troops for successful pursuit. That renegade white men are with them I have no doubt. I have a white man in the guard-house, who was found in possession of pocket-book, money, and papers of an emigrant, who is missing and believed to have been murdered. I am satisfied that the mail company and the Government would both be benefited by the change of routes at a proper time, and so wrote the Postmaster-General some weeks since. Then everything was quiet. Since that time the Indians have made hostile demonstrations, and I fear if the mail and all the troops leave this route the Indians will suppose they were frightened away, and will destroy the telegraph line and probably rob and murder such small parties as are not able to defend themselves. I have directed all the officers on the line to urge upon the emigrants the necessity of forming strong companies and exercising vigilance. In obedience to your order and the urgent calls of the mail company I sent the Utah troops to Bridger to guard the line from that post to Salt Lake, which leaves me only Colonel Collins, Sixth Ohio Cavalry, about 300 strong, and two skeleton companies of Fourth Regiment Cavalry, about 60 men, mounted upon horses purchased seven years ago, to protect the 400 miles intervening between this post and Fort Bridger. I need not say that this force cannot protect a line of such length unless the Indians are willing to behave well. I think I am doing all that can be done with so small a force mounted as they are and without any grain forage. My scouts inform me that a portion of the stolen property is now in an Indian Village on Beaver Creek but little more than 100 miles south of this post. It consists of 1,000 lodges, say 3,000 fighting men. I suppose I could whip these Indians if I could concentrate my command and go against them; but in the first place my troops are distributed along a line of 500 miles, and in the second place if I take the troops all away from the line the mail stock, telegraph line, and emigrants would be almost certain to suffer. I am therefore compelled to await re-enforcements, or at least until the emigration is out of danger. If a regiment of mounted troops could be sent by boat to Fort Pierre, [South Dakota,] which is only 300 miles north of this post, a joint campaign could be made against these tribes, which I think would result in giving peace to this region for years to come. Presuming it to be the intention of the Government to keep the troops somewhere in this region during the coming winter, I beg to urge the necessity of sending authority to procure hay for the animals, and also to send grain, or authority to purchase it, in Colorado. Unless the hay contract is let soon it will be difficult to procure it within reasonable distance. Parties here are anxious to furnish it at less figures than it cost last year. I omitted to say above that under your telegraphic order I have kept at this post the escort furnished by you to the Governor of Utah. I also sent to Denver City to inquire the number and description of troops in that vicinity, and received for answer that there were 4 officers and 6 privates all told. The troops ordered from California on this line have probably not started. They have not got as far east as Carson Valley.

This letter is already too long. I leave Lieutenant Wilcox to explain anything I have omitted.

I am, general, respectfully, your obedient servant,
Jas. Craig (Letters of 1862 Reveal Trouble 1943, 150–152)

Overland Trail 🚇 🚃
Albany, Carbon, Sweetwater, and Uinta Counties
In 1825 trappers with General William Ashley's fur brigade, including Jim Bridger, first traveled the route that would become the Overland Trail in 1862. John C. Frémont traveled portions of it in 1842, and Cherokees en route to California in 1849 followed a similar path across Wyoming.

In 1850 Captain Howard Stansbury, on an exploratory mission with Bridger as his guide, crossed the route and noted it was a shorter road for travelers between Fort Laramie and Fort Bridger than the Oregon Trail. Lieutenant F. T. Bryan established a military wagon road over Stansbury's route in 1856. General stage travel began in 1862.

Generally the Overland Trail overlays the Cherokee Trail and enters Wyoming from Colorado at Virginia Dale, along U. S. 287

The Overland Trail is still clearly visible on private land in Carbon County between the locations of the Sulphur Springs and Washakie Stations. (*Candy Moulton*)

south of Laramie. It crosses the Laramie Plains, passing near the site of Fort Sanders/Fort John Buford before heading west generally along a route that is now Interstate 80.

The period of heaviest use was between 1862 and 1869. After 1862, overland travelers, who earlier crossed Wyoming on the Oregon–California–Mormon Trails that went farther north along the North Platte and Sweetwater Rivers, took the Overland Trail to avoid conflict with Lakota, Cheyenne, and Arapaho Indians. Even so,

Indians from those tribes as well as the Ute nation conducted occasional raids along the Overland route.

Stage stations and major sites on the Overland Trail in Wyoming were, from east to west: Willow Springs, Big Laramie, Little Laramie, Cooper Creek, Rock Creek, Medicine Bow, Fort Halleck, Elk Mountain, Pass Creek, North Platte Crossing, Sage Creek, Pine Grove, Bridger's Pass, Sulphur Springs, Washakie, Duck Lake, Dug Springs (or Barrel Springs), Fort LaClede, Big Pond (a swing station), Big Bend, Black Butte, Point of Rocks (also called Rock Point or Almond Station), Salt Wells, Rock Springs, Green River, Lone Tree, Ham's Fork (South Bend Station), and Fort Bridger.

Pacific Springs / Pacific Springs Stage Station 〒 ♠ 🛖
Fremont County

Located west of South Pass, these springs were the first emigrants found after they crossed the Continental Divide. Because the divide was so gradual, it was only when they saw water flowing west that they knew they were in the Pacific drainage, hence the name Pacific Springs. By 1860 a stage station, that was also used by the Pony Express, had been built at the site. Sir Richard Burton notes: "[T]he shanty was a trifle more uncomfortable than the average; our only seat a kind of trestled plank, which suggested a certain obsolete military punishment called riding on a rail" (1862, 166).

In 1866, according to Burton and photographer William Henry Jackson, the place served as a trading post (Burton 1862, in Haines 1981, 237). Later there was a store and saloon, as well as a brothel or "hog ranch" at the area, and eventually men named Halter and Flick had the operation, building several structures, so it is often referred to as the Halter and Flick Ranch. The springs are on private land just off Wyoming Highway 28 about twenty-five miles east of Farson and less than a mile from an interpretive area developed by the U. S. Bureau of Land Management.

Parting of the Ways 〒 🛖
Sweetwater County

At this site, about fifteen miles northeast of present Farson on public land, the Sublette or Greenwood Cutoff veered away from the

At Parting of the Ways, travelers left the Oregon Trail. (*Candy Moulton*)

Oregon Trail. A highway marker and interpretive area adjacent to Wyoming Highway 28 refers to Parting of the Ways, though it is actually "False Parting of the Ways" as the true division point for the trails is farther west. Oregon Trail travelers first used the Sublette/Greenwood Cutoff, although Argonauts on their way to California after 1849 used it most heavily.

Pass Creek 🌲
Carbon County
Named in September 1850 by the Howard Stansbury Exploring Expedition, the Pass Creek area is located southeast of Walcott Junction and accessible via Carbon County Road 404.

Pass Creek Station 🚌
Carbon County
This swing station on the Overland Trail was located on the northeast side of Elk Mountain. Constructed of pine logs, it was around

twenty-five feet square with a dirt roof. George Launsberry was the station keeper in 1863 when Utes stole several mules. Launsberry, accompanied by men from Fort Halleck, struck out in pursuit of the raiding Indians, although he did not catch them. Later the Indians brought the mules to Fort Halleck, offering to return them for a "reward" of $5 for each animal.

Captain Aspah Allen writes of those events:

> On the 19th [February 1863], a report came to me that the Ute Indians had broken up the station at Pass Creek, driven off the mail stock, cut up the harness, and committed other depredations. I started Lieutenant Brandley, with all the available force here (not having but 20 horses at the post), after them. He overtook and killed some of them, and was badly wounded by a ball through the left arm. He shot the Indian through the head. I brought my herd of horses in and went out myself, and hunted the hounds three days (Allen 1863, as quoted in Erb et al. 1989, 60).

The exact location of this station is not known, but it is likely on private ranch land.

Perkins Dinner Station
Carbon County
This station was on the Rawlins to Baggs stage and freight road.

Peryam Roadhouse
Carbon County
William T. and Alice Peryam established the large two-story Peryam Roadhouse, located just east of Riverside beside the Encampment River, to serve travelers and business men involved in the Grand Encampment Copper District mining boom. The Peryams had moved to the area in 1879, claiming homestead land. After discovery of minor amounts of gold and massive amounts of copper in 1896 and 1897, the influx of miners established a need for services such as meals and beds. The Peryams first housed people in their own home, then they built the roadhouse in 1899, charging 35 cents for a meal. At the time, the river had no bridge, so in 1901 Peryam constructed

the first toll bridge, charging two bits (25 cents) for a team and wagon and ten cents for a single rider.

The white two-story roadhouse with its green trim and long porch had nine upstairs bedrooms and a kitchen, parlor, and large dining room on the ground-floor level. Other buildings included the original Peryam house, other structures they had moved in, and such outbuildings as a granary, a chicken house, livestock barns, and a root cellar. The green trim has long since faded and the roof is beginning to sag, but the roadhouse remains standing beside the river. It is on private land but can be seen from Wyoming Highway 230.

Portugee Phillips' Ride 🚏
Johnson, Campbell, Converse, Platte, and Goshen Counties
One of the incredible horseback rides in the annals of Wyoming military history took place on a bitter cold night December 21, 1866, when John "Portugee" Phillips and Daniel Dixon undertook a harrowing journey from Fort Phil Kearny in north-central Wyoming to Fort Laramie. They sought reinforcements after the deaths of Lieutenant William J. Fetterman and his entire command when the soldiers were lured from the fort, attacked, and killed by Lakota warriors led by Red Cloud.

A full moon shone that night as Phillips and Dixon rode from Fort Phil Kearny. Phillips is given the most credit for the ride by Wyoming historians. He rode first to Fort Reno, then continued to Horseshoe Station along the North Platte River before finally arriving at Fort Laramie. Dixon likely left Fort Phil Kearny at a different time from Phillips, but the two joined forces before they reached Horseshoe Station. It is unclear whether Dixon and possibly other men accompanied Phillips to Fort Laramie from Horseshoe Station, but Phillips rode the last leg of the 235-mile journey that ended at Old Bedlam in Fort Laramie on Christmas Eve night.

Upon receiving confirmation of the Fetterman battle, or massacre as non-Indians sometimes call it, Colonel I. N. Palmer at Fort Laramie sent reinforcements to Fort Reno and Fort Phil Kearny. Those troops reached Fort Reno on January 11, 1867, and within five days were at Fort Phil Kearny. (*See also* Fetterman Fight.)

Artist M. D. Houghton's depicted the arrival of John "Portugee" Phillips at Horseshoe Station with his message of the killing of Lieutenant William J. Fetterman's command in December 1866. (*Courtesy of Wyoming State Museum*)

Pine Grove Station
Carbon County

This was a home station on the Overland Trail located at the foot of Miller Hill near Pine Grove Creek. The station had a large log building with several rooms where women slept, which also served as the kitchen and dining room. There was also a log bunkhouse for male travelers, a barn, and a blacksmith shop (Carley 1961a).

In 1892 the *Saratoga Sun* ran an account by Joe J. Hurt of a stagecoach journey and Indian attack that took place west of Pine Grove:

> I was there [at North Platte Crossing] in June 1865, and the station then had been cut off from communications with Sulphur Springs, west of us, for three weeks by Indians.
>
> Mail after mail came in for the west until a great pile of it accumulated. One day our superintendent decided to make a night run and get the mail through. That night three big coaches and two big cages were filled full of mailsacks, and six horses were attached to each. . . . It was 11

o'clock at night when we started out and we were off like the wind. The night was a beautiful one with a full moon.

Our nerves were wrought up to a high pitch as we bowled along over the hard roads. . . . About 3 o'clock in the morning we passed Pine Grove station, where the man in charge had been killed, the station burned, and the stock stolen sometime previous. It was a suggestive remnant of what might soon be our fate.

Nothing had yet happened to us as day began to break, and we began to be hopeful that we would yet make it without trouble. Vain hope!

We had as a driver of one of the coaches a young man whose name I have forgotton, . . . but who went by the name of 'Heenan' on account of his great strength and courage. . . .

Our road went up through a narrow canyon several miles long; the walls of which rose gently upward on either side to about 100 yards from the roadway. As we were driving through this, just after day break, the Indians opened fire on us from either side. At the first volley two or three of our men were killed and it was a running fight from there to the top of the canyon. At one time it looked as though Heenan's outfit was gone. I saw an Indian with a colts revolver in his hands, lying prone on the bank of the canyon, his elbows resting on the ground taking deliberate aim at Heenan. The Indian saw he had not made enough allowance for the motion of the stage, and mended his aim sufficiently that the sixth bullet broke Heenan's right arm above the elbow. It fell helpless at his side but nothing daunted, he caught all the lines in his left hand and never slacked his pace. . . .

The sun was just rising as we gained the head of the canyon and drove out on the level prairies. In hardly more time than it takes to tell it, we formed a corral of our coaches, placed the horses inside it, piled the mail sacks into a circular breastwork, and prepared to sell our lives as dearly as possible. . . .

What a horrible day that was! A hot, broiling sun, not water or shelter, and our little party surrounded by approximately 500 hooting, yelling, murderous savages, who all day long, without intermission, rode around and around us, raining arrows and bullets on us like hail. When any of our men were killed, their bodies were piled up on top of the mail sacks to help keep out the bullets. It was hard, but it was necessary. . . .

About sundown the red devils pulled off, and seemed to be inclined to give up the fight . . . when they withdrew at sundown, Heenan said, 'Up now and let's get out of this. Hitch up the horses, throw in the mail and we'll make another try at getting to Sulphur Springs.' We flew at it and were soon ready to travel. . . . [W]e drove like the wind . . . The Indians did not attack again until we were about a mile and a half from Sulphur Springs Station, when they opened another bombardment.

It was down hill to the station and we kept going as fast as we could. Meanwhile the men at the station heard the fighting going on, and when they rode out to take part, the Indians again retreated (Running the Gauntlet 1892).

Plant's Station
Natrona County
This station near Devil's Gate midway between Rawlins and Casper on Wyoming Highway 220 served the Pony Express as a relay point. (*See* Pony Express Trail.)

Platte Bridge, Battle of, 1865
(*See* Platte Bridge Station.)

Platte Bridge Station
Natrona County
This important site, a log structure built in 1859 at the crossing of the North Platte River in present Casper, served as a Pony Express station and was also a military station to protect the transcontinental

Frontier artist William Henry Jackson's depicted Platte Bridge Station. (*Courtesy National Park Service*)

telegraph that later became Fort Caspar (*see entry*). The Pony Express called it North Platte Station. It protected travelers on the Oregon–California–Mormon Trail, and the men stationed at the site kept communications open along the overland routes. The post, later known as Fort Caspar, was garrisoned until 1867.

Sergeant Isaac Pennock was stationed at Platte Bridge Station in 1865 as tension rose all across the region in a year that became known as the "Bloody Year on the Plains," and he left these diary entries:

> May 27—Have news that the Indians attacked Rocky Ridge [St. Mary's, near South Pass] today in strong force.

> May 28—Hear the Indians crossed the Platte River in front of our provision train. [Colonel Thomas] Moonlight has sent reinforcements to the train and a dispatch to Colonel Plumb to send a detachment also from this end of the road. No telegraph communication further east than Deer Creek, not west of Sweetwater [Station].

> June 3—At 3 p.m. received dispatch from Colonel Plumb that Indians have attacked station at Upper Bridge; ordered to cross lower bridge with 20 men and attack them in the rear. Captain James E. Greer and 20 men started, but the

Indians were gone when we got there, but plenty of fresh tracks. Colonel Plumb is in close pursuit, and was in fighting distance at two hours before sundown. We have heard from the fight; two of our men killed and one Indian and several ponies. One of our men had ten arrows shot into him; scalped and fingers cut off and terrible mangled.

June 28—Fight on Reshaw Creek.

July 7—[Major Mackey telegraphed Captain Greer to send ten men to Sweetwater 55 miles west of Platte Bridge to repair the telegraph line.] Which order was almost equivalent to an order to march that number of men to shoot them down, scalp them, cut off their hands and feet, cut out their hearts, liver, sinew and send them to the savages. The boys refused to go unless 30 men were sent (Pennock 1865).

The tension and conflicts continued until July 25 when events took a decidedly hostile turn near Platte Bridge.

As many as three hundred to five hundred Lakota warriors led by Red Cloud, Old-Man-Afraid-Of-His-Horses, and Young-Man-Afraid-Of-His-Horses and Cheyenne warriors following Roman Nose, Dull Knife, and White Bull gathered near the Platte River in late July 1865. Some of the warriors had been harassing troops and cutting wires of the transcontinental telegraph in the region west of Deer Creek for most of the summer. On July 25 some Indians rode toward the post at Platte Bridge. A few soldiers went out from the post to meet the Indians, engaging in a skirmish that had little effect on fighters from either side, but the soldiers did not follow the Indians over the hills as the Indians had hoped they would.

At the same time, Sergeant Amos J. Custard, Eleventh Kansas Cavalry, was en route from Sweetwater Station at Independence Rock with three mule-drawn wagons. The evening of July 25, Custard's train camped midway between Sweetwater Station and Platte Bridge Station at Willow Creek, a campsite that had been used for years by overland emigrants. As Custard set camp, Lieutenant Henry Clay Bretney went on ahead to Platte Bridge so the soldiers there would know the wagons were on their way.

At dawn July 26, Custard had the wagon train on the move over the telegraph and emigrant road, intending to push the final fifteen miles to the post at Platte Bridge. Shortly after breakfast, troops at Platte Bridge Station saw around ninety Indians on the hill a couple of miles from the post. After rejecting other alternatives, Major Martin Anderson ordered Lieutenant Caspar Collins, Sergeant Adolph Hankhammer, Sergeant Isaac Pennock, and Corporal Henry Grimm of the Eleventh Ohio Volunteer Cavalry to take twenty-five men, including representatives of Companies I and K, Eleventh Kansas Volunteer Cavalry, to leave the station and head toward Custard's oncoming wagon train. As they prepared to leave, Collins borrowed two pistols from Lieutenant Bretney.

The relief troops rode over the Platte Bridge and were still in sight of the station when Lakota and Cheyenne Indians swooped around the troops, cutting off any retreat. A short fight, lasting only about ten minutes, ended with the deaths of several soldiers, including Collins.

Sergeant Pennock (1865) describes the fight:

> July 26—Terrible day for our command, and no knowing how it will end. . . . We crossed the bridge and got about one mile from camp, when from the Northeast and Southwest and every point of the compass, the savages came. It appeared as though they sprung up out of the ground. They completely surrounded us. There was no alternative. Death was approaching on every side in its most horrible form— that of the tomahawk and scalping knife of the Indians. We turned and charged into the thickest of them, drawing our pistols and doing the best we could. It was a terrible ordeal to go through. It was really running the gauntlet for dear life. After a terrible break-neck race of ¼ of a mile, we arrived at the bridge, where the boys had run out to our support. In the charge we lost about five killed and about twelve wounded. Lieutenant Collins was killed. Everything was in full view of the station.

The events of the day had not ended, however. Not long after the fight in which Collins died, Sergeant Custard came over the hill with his wagons, apparently unaware of the danger. Four men riding in advance of the wagons saw the Indians and raced to safety at the post. Three of the men made it to the post, but the Indians killed the other rider.

Upon seeing the Indians, Custard put his wagons in a corral formation and set up a defense. The Indians attacked the wagons in force. Pennock (1865) writes:

> All this we could plainly see from the station, but we could do nothing for them. . . . We could see the Indians in swarms charge down on our boys when they would roll volley after volley into them, it seems as though the boys were in a strong position, twenty in all being their number.

Before nightfall the Indians killed all the men remaining with Custard; a couple had managed to escape as the attack began. Troops sent out to repair the telegraph line east of Platte Bridge so a message could be sent to outside troops of the troubles were also attacked. Those troops made it back to the station safely, but from the attack on July 26 until July 1, Platte Bridge Station was cut off from outside help. The telegraph line could not be repaired because of constant threat of attack by the Indians.

But help eventually came. Pennock's entry of August 1 reads, "At four o'clock the joyful word came 'The Line is Working.' The joyful tick, tick, tick put a glad smile on every face. Soon heard the Sixth Michigan Cavalry would be here tomorrow" (1865).

In the aftermath, Platte Bridge Station was renamed Fort Caspar, for Lieutenant Caspar Collins. The city that grew at the site later is also named for Collins, though the spelling is Casper.[6] The Civilian Conservation Corps rebuilt Fort Caspar at the original site, and it is now a National Historic Site managed by the City of Casper.

Point of Rocks Cemetery and Register
Sweetwater County

To the west of Point of Rocks Station, just south of Interstate 80 at Point of Rocks, is a small nineteenth century cemetery, apparently holding the remains of people murdered in a stage robbery, although

The Point of Rocks Station is now a Wyoming State Historic Site located just south of the railroad tracks at Point of Rocks. The stretch of the Cherokee Trail at Point of Rocks is clearly marked and easily accessible to explore on foot. (*Candy Moulton*)

details about the robbery and their identities are not known. This cemetery was fenced in recent years as part of a Boy Scout project.

Point of Rocks Station
Sweetwater County
The stone Point of Rocks Station that served the Overland Trail is now a Wyoming Historic Site, located just south of Interstate 80 at Point of Rocks. It is also known as Rock Point Station and Almond Station. The station became a primary supply point for the gold mines at South Pass City. Located just south of the Union Pacific rail line, the station was a gateway to the mining district. Miners departed the train here before heading overland to the gold district, and freighters made routine trips from the railroad to the mining towns to the north. Later the station was an important livestock shipping point for animals moving to or from markets in Omaha and Chicago.

Pony Express Trail 🚃

Goshen, Platte, Converse, Natrona, Carbon, Fremont, Sweetwater, Uinta, and Lincoln Counties

William Russell, Alexander Majors, and William Waddell established the Pony Express to carry mail between St. Joseph, Missouri, and Sacramento, California, in 1860. The role of the Pony Express was to link the nation at a time of increasing national concern over pending conflict in the Civil War. The first Pony Express messenger rode from St. Joe on April 3, 1860, and the final ride occurred October 24, 1861. The express service was put out of business by the construction of the transcontinental telegraph.

Following the route of the California Trail across northeast Kansas, along the Blue River into Nebraska, then along the Platte River and North Platte River into Wyoming, the Pony Boys, as the riders became known, served from a number of stations located roughly twenty miles apart. Stations were two basic types: home stations, where riders lived and stayed when they were not riding their routes, and change, relay, or swing stations. At home stations, horses could receive extra care such as medical attention or the services of a farrier, if needed. The change, relay, or swing stations had only basic amenities and extra horses. At those sites, riders dismounted quickly, removed from their horse the leather saddle covering—called a mochila—that had letters and dispatches in locked pouches, placed it over the saddle on a new horse and rode out quickly along the trail. Both types of stations had station tenders, but the home stations also had cooks to prepare meals and space for lodging.

The Pony Express was short-lived, lasting only until completion of the transcontinental telegraph line, but it served the important purpose of maintaining communications before the outbreak of the Civil War. The enterprise was a financial disaster for Russell, Majors, and Waddell. Officially known as the Central Overland California & Pikes Peak Express Company, it soon had the nickname the Clean Out of Cash and Poor Pay.

The following were the Pony Express stations in Wyoming, from east to west: Cold Springs Station (also called Spring Ranch, Torrington, and Junction House), Bordeaux (also called Beauvais), Fort Laramie, Nine Mile (also known as Sand Point, Central Star and

This drawing by M. D. Houghton shows the exchange of the Pony Express mochila at a station in Wyoming. (*Courtesy of Wyoming State Museum*)

Ward's), Cottonwood, Horseshoe (a home station managed by Jack Slade), Elk Horn, LaBonte, Bed Tick, LaPrele, Box Elder, Deer Creek, Little Muddy (Rock in the Glen or Glen Rock), Bridger, Platte Bridge (North Platte River), Red Buttes, Willow Springs, Horse Creek, Sweetwater (Independence Rock, a rough cabin with bunks for riders and a horse shed but no corral), Devil's Gate, Plant's, Split Rock, Three Crossings (the home station of Bill Cody), Ice Slough, Warm Springs, St. Mary's (also called Rocky Ridge, probably a home station), Rock Creek, South Pass (also known as Burnt Ranch and Upper Sweetwater Station), Pacific Springs, Dry Sandy, Little Sandy, Big Sandy, Big Bend (also called Big Timber or Simpson's Hollow), Green River (a home station), Michael Martin's, Ham's Fork (South Bend), Church Buttes, Millersville, Fort Bridger, Muddy Creek, Quaking Asp Springs (also known as Aspen Station or Spring Station), and Bear River (*see individual entries*).

Portuguese Houses 🛶
Johnson County

Antonio Matéo, working with Benjamin L. E. Bonneville, started this trading establishment, which was referred to as both Portuguese Houses and Fort Antonio. The hewn-log cabins were constructed in 1834. The complex was surrounded by a two-hundred-foot-square log stockade. Trappers brought furs to the post and traded them for supplies; the pelts were subsequently bundled for shipment to eastern markets. The trading houses were in use from 1834 until 1839. They were on the Upper Powder River, but the exact location is uncertain.

A description of the site in 1859 by Captain W. F. Raynolds in his "Report on the Exploration of the Yellowstone River" notes that the cabins were "badly dilapidated and only one side of the pickets remains standing. These, however, are of hewn logs, and from their character it is evident that the structures were originally very strongly built" (Brown 1969, 118).

Post at Platte Bridge 🏳
Natrona County

This post was established in 1855 as Camp Davis and later renamed Camp Payne in 1858 before becoming Post at Platte Bridge also in 1858. It was located in present Evansville near the Richard, or Reshaw, Bridge and should not be confused with Platte Bridge Station, located a few miles to the west and upstream on the North Platte River.

Powder River Expedition, 1876 🏳
Brigadier General George Crook organized the Powder River Expedition of 1876 that involved fighting in Wyoming's Powder River Basin in early June, including the Battle of the Rosebud. Crook withdrew his troops after that fight to a location on Goose Creek and was not involved in the Battle of the Little Bighorn on June 25 (*see* Crook Campaign, 1876). Subsequent to Little Bighorn, Crook's troops traveled across northeastern Wyoming and into the Dakotas, were involved in the fight at Slim Buttes, and eventually traveled to Fort Robinson in northwest Nebraska.

Crook took to the field again in the fall of 1876, leading a winter campaign against Cheyenne and Lakota tribesmen that included the attack on November 25, 1876, on the Cheyenne Village of Dull Knife (*see* Dull Knife Battle). Troops involved in the winter campaign organized at Fort Fetterman, established a staging area at Cantonment Reno (later Fort McKinney), and spent time in camp along the Powder River and Belle Fourche River before eventually withdrawing to Fort Fetterman for dispersal to other locations.

Prospect Hill ♠ 🚙
Natrona County

Also called Ryan Hill, this landmark was the last major hill emigrants had to ascend before getting their first glimpse of Independence Rock and the Sweetwater Mountains. Of significance, Prospect Hill is also one location where one can still see the original route of the transcontinental telegraph in the form of a grade between Willow Springs at the bottom and the pinnacle of Prospect Hill.

The area is accessible by following Natrona County Road 319, also known as Oregon Trail Road, where it takes off of Wyoming Highway 220 about twelve miles northeast of Independence Rock. A U.S. Bureau of Land Management interpretive area is near Prospect Hill. From that interpretive area, continue northeast on Road 319 until the road connects with Poison Spider Road, then follow that road (also called Natrona County Road 201) to the north and west, eventually to Casper. This route follows the basic path of the Oregon–Mormon–California trails and passes near such landmarks as Horse Creek Pony Express Station and Avenue of Rocks, or Emigrant Gap. For trail maps and information, contact the National Historic Trails Interpretive Center or Fort Caspar National Historic Place in Casper.

Quaking Asp Springs Station 🚙
Uinta County

This Pony Express relay station was also called Aspen Station or Spring Station. (*See* Pony Express Trail.)

Rawhide Buttes Station 🚂
Niobrara County
This station on the Cheyenne to Black Hills (Deadwood) stage route, about fifteen miles south of the Running Water Stage Station and the present town of Lusk, also served as a U. S. mail distribution center.

Rawlins and Gold Hill Stage Line 🚂
Carbon County
Brothers James and Joe Rankin operated this stage line between Rawlins and the mining district at Gold Hill in the Medicine Bow Mountains east of Saratoga beginning in 1892. James Rankin had been a Carbon County sheriff who was involved in the arrest of Big Nose George Parrott (*see* Elk Mountain, Attack on Wyoming Lawmen), while Joe Rankin made a reputation when he rode for help after Utes attacked troops from Fort Fred Steele in the Milk Creek Battle in northwestern Colorado in 1879. This stage line later became known as the Rawlins and Saratoga Stage Line when it provided service between those two communities.

Rawlins Spring 🌲 🚂
Carbon County
As engineers laid out the route of the Union Pacific Railroad, they established sites for stations located roughly twenty miles apart. The spring General John A. Rawlins discovered in a draw while engineering the route of the Union Pacific Railroad was the best of any location he could find at the end of one of those twenty-mile stretches. When General Grenville Dodge reached the location in 1868, he named the site Rawlins Spring. The spring is located just north of the present city of Rawlins.

Rawlins to Baggs Stage and Freight Road 🚂
Carbon County
The road ranches and stations on this road between Rawlins and Baggs were Sixteen Mile Station, Twenty Mile Station, Sulphur Springs Station (also a station on the Overland Trail), Willows Station, Perkins Dinner Station, Muddy Bridge Station, or Jerry's Place, Jumbo Station, and Baggs.

William F. Raynolds Explorations, 1859–1860 🚣 🏴

This Corps of Topographical Engineers expedition led by Captain William F. Raynolds involved explorations of the Powder River region to determine the location for a future military road. Captain Raynolds mapped the area so accurately in 1859 and 1860 that the maps served as the foundation for all military maps in the region during the 1870s Plains Indian Wars (Rosenberg 1989). (*See also* Maynadier Expedition, 1859–1860.)

Red Buttes, Battle of 🏴 🏴
Natrona County

A marker denoting this July 1865 fight between Cheyenne and Lakota warriors and a wagon train led by Sergeant Amos Custard is located along Wyoming Highway 220 four miles southwest of Fort Caspar. During the fight Lieutenant Caspar Collins and four men died, while eighteen men with a wagon train led by Sergeant Custard also were attacked and killed. (*See* Platte Bridge Station for details about the fight.)

Red Buttes Mail Station 🚌
Natrona County

Known as U. S. Mail Station No. 28, the Red Buttes Mail Station was on the west bank of the North Platte River about a dozen miles southwest of Casper on U. S. 220 and likely near the Oregon Trail/Red Buttes marker placed beside that road not far from Bessemer Bend. This station also served as a Pony Express relay station from 1860 to 1861.

"Heck" Reel Wagon Train Fight 🚌 ⛺
Platte County

Teamster George Throstle led a freight wagon train owned by A. H. "Heck" Reel, a contractor and early Cheyenne mayor, from Cheyenne north toward Fort Fetterman in July 1876. At the divide between Elkhorn and LaBonte Creeks on July 8, Cheyenne and Lakota Indians attacked Throstle and his assistant Sylvester Sherman as they rode ahead of the wagons. Although Throstle was killed, Sherman made a run back toward the sixteen wagons, which were circled for defense. A few of the wagons filled with bacon, whiskey, and beer were not able to reach the circle and Indians attacked them, sampling some of the goods before setting them on fire. The men abandoned the slow wagons and reached safety with their companions, holding the Indians at bay until the tribesmen finally retreated. Wagon boss Throstle was the only teamster killed, although another was injured. The Indians also killed some horses and oxen belonging to the wagon train. There is no record of any injuries or deaths among the Indians.

On August 3, 1876, the *Cheyenne Daily Leader* reports on the attack, quoting a telegram sent on August 2 to A. H. Reel by John Hunton at Fort Laramie:

> The Indians attacked your train near Elkhorn, yesterday about four o'clock.
>
> They killed and scalped Geo. Throstle, wounded a teamster, killed four horses, ten oxen, and burned three wagons.
>
> Sam Graves and Geo. Powell broght Throstle's body into this fort to-night. Your train is on the Labonte to-night.

The paper adds:

> George Throstle was a man who was esteemed highly of his numerous friends here. . . . He was master of the train, which was conveying Government freight to Fetterman, and had sixteen men under his command, all of whom were armed and certainly made a desperate fight.
>
> Mr. Throstle had been in Reel's employ for nine years, was about 35 years old, and was faithful, industrious and temperate (*Cheyenne Daily Leader* 1876).

In later years Sherman wrote an account of the attack, although his details differ from the first reports by the *Daily Leader*.

> On the 5th day of July 1876, we commenced to hire men and load up with government freight for Fort Fetterman. We had to hire all kinds of men from good bull-whackers and Mexicans down to a few long haired Missourians.

Mr. Reel was there and told Throstle to furnish every man with a good forty-five sixshooter, and a forty-four Winchester, and have them carry the guns in the jocky box on the front end of the wagon, as there was plenty of Indian signs along the North Platte river. . . .

The hill at was a long hard hill, and both Throstle and I stayed back until the last wagon was up it. Each wagon had one trail wagon and some had two. After we got up the hill, we rode out ahead of the teams to look over the road. When we were about 300 yards away from the lead team . . . it seemed that a hundred Indians jumped out of a draw shooting at us. Three bullets struck Throstle while only one struck me. [Sherman made a run for the wagon train.] I had no time to shoot as I used both feet and both hands to whip [the horse] with. . . . all the good men were driving the lead teams and knew what to do and in a short time we were corralled. In the meantime the men were each shooting at [the Indians] with a six shooter, as they came up closer. One man jumped on a wagon and began to throw off sacks of flour while others commenced to build bre[a]stworks.

A Mexican was driving the next to the last wagon and a long haired Missourian the last team. The Missourian saw that there was no show [possibility] to get his team in [to the corral of other wagons] so [he] left it and came on up to the Mexican's [who had deserted at the first of the fighting and crawled in among the drygoods in one of the lead wagons] and whacked it on in. It looked for a while as if the Indians would get him but he shot with one hand and whacked the bulls with the other. After we got in a few good rounds with our guns they fell back and would only come up in sight. We laid there all day, and as night came on they came up to the wagon which was left on the outside, at about three hundred yards distance, that was loaded with ten thousand pounds of bacon, and forty kegs of beer, and threw off the beer and rolled it down a long hill and set the bacon on fire. The blaze seemed to reach two hundred feet high. . . .

The next morning [the Indians had departed so] we unyoked our oxen and drove them back to Elkhorn to water, while others went to hunt for the teams that were hitched to the wagon [that had been burned]. The wheel oxen were burned to death, and the next team was burned some, but they had pulled the front wheels out from the wagon [to get away from the fire], and five teams were grazing around still hitched [yoked] together (Shaw 1926, 177–180).

Register Cliff ⌁ ♣ 🛒
Platte County
Travelers on the emigrant road to Oregon, California, and Utah often camped near the North Platte River at a large sandstone bluff upon which they carved their names and the dates of their travel. Register Cliff is now a Wyoming State Historic Site located three miles southeast of Guernsey via road 109S.

Richard/Reshaw Bridge ⌁ 🛒
Natrona County
In 1851 John Baptiste Richard (pronounced Reshaw) built a bridge over the North Platte River in the vicinity of Deer Creek to serve traffic on the Oregon–California Trail. A spring flood took out that bridge in 1852, so Richard built a new structure over the river in what is now Evansville. This bridge across the North Platte River in present Evansville served Oregon and California Trail travelers after its construction in 1853. Richard, whose name is often written as Reshaw for the phonetic spelling of his name, charged fifty cents for a person or animal to cross and five dollars for a team and wagon. In 1860 Sir Richard Burton traveled the trail and writes:

> After about two hours of hot sun, we debouched upon the bank of the Platte, at a spot where one was the Lower Ferry. The river bed here is full of holes and quicksands, and the stream is so cold and swift, that many have been drowned when bathing, more when attempting to save time by fording

This replica of the Richard/Reshaw Bridge abutment at the North Platte Crossing on the Oregon Trail is in Evansville. The trail entry to the river is visible on the far side of the river. (*Courtesy Wyoming State Historic Preservation Office*)

> it. A wooden bridge was built at this point some years ago . . .
> by one Reshaw (Burton 1862; reprint 1990, 140).

The 1853 bridge remained in use at least periodically through 1865. A recreation of it has been built in an Evansville Town Park adjacent to the North Platte River.

Robber's Roost Station 🚂 🚃
Niobrara County

This station on the Cheyenne–Deadwood stage route was located about three miles north of present day Mule Creek Junction. Nearby, at a site where U.S. 85 crosses the Cheyenne River north of Lusk, robbers often lay in wait for wagon trains and stagecoaches. They knew because of the terrain at the approach to the river that the stagecoaches would move more slowly here than at other places on the route. An article at the time in the *Cheyenne Daily Leader* expresses outrage at the continued attacks on the mail deliveries:

> A war of extermination should be waged against them until the last robber is laid low; and the United States army cannot be employed to a better purpose than to aid the civil authorities in an offensive campaign against the outlaws, whether they may be found robbing the mails, stealing horses, or robbing our settlers and freighters traveling along the public highway (Wyoming Recreation Commission 1988, 187).

Rock Creek Station 🛖 🚂
Albany County

This station, which served the Overland Trail and the trail to Fort Fetterman, had a number of buildings, including a warehouse, a blacksmith shop, a general store, a mess hall, three saloons, and two hotels as well as stockyards. Joe Bush filed a homestead claim in the area and operated the stage station. He also built a toll bridge across Rock Creek. Occasionally there were incidents with Indians who were possibly Ute, Arapaho, Cheyenne, or Lakota, as all four tribes ranged in the area routinely.

In 1865 J. Zimmer emigrated over the Overland Trail. In *Across the Plains by Immigrant Wagon*, he writes, "The place Rock Creek consisted of the station buildings, a small store and five or six houses and had the appearance and business activity of a small village" (Erb et al. 1989, 45).

Bush's homestead claim passed to Sadie and Bill Williams, who continued operating the station. The couple also planted a large garden to provide fresh produce. After Bill's death, Sadie managed the place alone. Eventually she remarried and sold the property. The best-known operator of Rock Creek Station was Alvy Dixon, who had been a freighter between Fort McKinney, Fort Fetterman, and Rock Creek.

A stage line began operating out of Rock Creek Station, running north over the Fetterman Trail and eventually connecting with the Bozeman Trail and extending on to Junction City, Montana. The route was also used heavily to move cattle herds transported by train to Rock Creek Station then trailed overland to northern Wyoming and Montana ranges. Cattle from the north were also taken south for shipment to markets in the East. In the fall of 1883, there were reports of one hundred carloads of cattle shipped from the station every day. Rock Creek Station was abandoned by the Union Pacific Railroad on April 1, 1900. The station subsequently passed to Dixon's stepson, Chet Pitcher. The property remains in the Pitcher family's possession and is in the town of Arlington, which grew up after the heyday of stagecoach and cattle trails.

Rock Creek Station
Fremont County
This station served as a Pony Express relay station in 1860 and 1861. (*See* Pony Express Trail.)

Rock Dale
Albany County
Located near the site of the Rock Creek Station that served the Overland Trail west of Laramie, Rock Dale was a post office established in 1882.

Rock in the Glen
Converse County
This popular Oregon Trail emigrant campground, also called Glen Rock Station or Little Muddy Station, served as a Pony Express station in 1860 and 1861.

Rock Point Station
Sweetwater County
This is another name for Point of Rocks Station, located on the Overland and Cherokee Trails (*see individual entries*).

Rock Springs, Chinese Massacre
Sweetwater County
Mountain man Jim Bridger is credited with first spotting the coal seams in the Rock Springs area. Mining activities started in the late

Chinese workers helped construct the Union Pacific track across Wyoming and later worked in Union Pacific coal mines in Rock Springs, where, in 1885, numerous Chinese were killed or driven from their homes during a riot. (*Courtesy Wyoming State Archives*)

1860s after the Union Pacific Railroad built through the region. The coal mining activities in this area, and farther east in Carbon County near the town of Carbon, were necessary to the operation of the Union Pacific, as the coal provided power for the steam-fired train engines.

In the fall of 1875, miners, who had organized in unions, struck for higher wages. The Union Pacific responded by firing union organizers. The company knew it could keep all coal-fired trains operating so long as the mines remained in production, so it was a tremendous blow on November 8, 1875, when around 500 miners walked off the job at both Carbon and Rock Springs. The striking miners threatened to start fires in the coal seams at Rock Springs, prompting Union Pacific officials to request military intervention. Governor John Thayer sent troops who took up defensive positions around the Rock Springs coal mines. The standoff continued for two weeks as miners watched their resources, such as food and money, dwindle. Then the Union Pacific kicked up the tension when the company hired 150 Chinese miners who quickly set up a camp near the Rock Springs No. 3 Mine as they began working the mines. Governor Thayer warned the striking miners not to interfere with the Chinese workers, telling them that he would call on more military troops if necessary.

On November 25, 1875, the *Laramie Daily Sentinel* reported that the situation in Rock Springs had eased. A few days later the troops pulled out of Rock Springs. Some striking miners went back to work alongside the Chinese laborers, and for the next ten years few problems were reported. The tranquility was shattered on September 2, 1885, when a labor riot broke out between white and Chinese miners. White aggressors took control of the Rock Springs Chinatown, burning homes and attacking and killing the Chinese residents. More than two dozen Chinese residents lost their lives in the rioting; many were forced from their homes with scant clothing, taking refuge on the wind-whipped desert land outside the city.

President Grover Cleveland ordered federal troops to Rock Springs; they remained in place for the next thirteen years until they were recalled to take part in the Spanish-American War. No further significant incidents occurred at the mines involving Chinese miners. Although a grand jury convened to consider charges in the wake of the September 1885 massacre of Chinese residents in Rock Springs, no one was indicted.

Rock Springs Station
Sweetwater County

In 1860, a Pony Express rider seeking to elude Indians found the springs located in the rocks that gave this area its name. There was an Overland Trail station known as Rock Springs. The trail station predated the city of the same name by nearly a decade.

Rocky Ridge
Fremont County

Overland travelers had a difficult time negotiating the relatively steep, rocky slope as they pulled away from the Sweetwater River Valley and headed west to South Pass. The ridge the travelers crossed became known as Rocky Ridge for its terrain.

In 1842 John C. Frémont traveled through the area, writing:

On either side of the valley, which is four or five miles broad, the mountains rise. . . . On the south side the range is timbered. On the north . . . granite masses rise abruptly from the green swale of the river, terminating in a line of broken summits. Except in the crevices of the rock and here and there on a ledge or bench of mountain, where a few hardy pines have clustered together, they are perfectly bare and destitute of vegetation. Among these masses, where there are sometimes isolated hills and ridges, green valleys open in upon the river, which sweeps the base of these mountains for 36 miles (Frémont 1845, as quoted in Moulton 1995, 240).

When the Mormon handcart company led by James Grey Willie reached this area in mid-October 1856, it was snowing and cold. Struggling in bitter temperatures as they climbed out of the Sweetwater Valley pulling their carts, the members of the Willie Company suffered severely, many experiencing frozen extremities, as they jolted carts over the shelf rock of the hillside and ridge.

Rocky Ridge is east of Atlantic City on public land managed by the U. S. Bureau of Land Management. Use restrictions are in place to protect the site. For information, contact the BLM in Lander.

Running Water Stage Station 🚙
Niobrara County
Located near the present community of Lusk, Running Water Stage Station was a stop on the Cheyenne to Black Hills (Deadwood) stage route from 1876 to 1887. It became a frontier community in its own right until the Chicago–Northwestern Railroad decided that its main terminal would be at Lusk. After that decision, Running Water declined in prominence. The region between the Running Water Station and the Rawhide Buttes Station, fifteen miles to the south, is listed on the National Register of Historic Places.

Ryan Hill 🌲 🚙
Natrona County
(*See* Prospect Hill and Willow Springs Station.)

Sage Creek Station 🛻 ▦
Carbon County

This station on the Overland Trail was located on the northeast bank of Miller Creek, in spite of its name. Located on public land, the site of Sage Creek Station is south of Rawlins. The log building was approximately twenty-five by sixty feet with an adobe fireplace and dirt and pole roof. A log corral connected to the building on the north and east sides. As with other stations in this area in 1865, emigrants and soldiers assigned to the region recorded numerous Indian attacks. Nevada Cavalry Lieutenant Brown reports an incident that took place June 8, 1865:

> The detachment at Sage Creek station was attacked by about 100 Indians. After one hour's severe fighting they were compelled to evacuate in consequence of a deficiency in ammunition. . . . The moment they left the station they were completely surrounded. There ensued a desperate fight; the detachment retreated toward Pine Grove Station. The Indians followed for eight miles, killing George Bodine and Perry Stewart, wounding and capturing Orland Ducket, wounding Corp. W. H. Caldwell and Private William Wilson, all of Company K, 11th Ohio Volunteer Cavalry. . . . Corporal Caldwell and Private Wilson escaped to Pine Grove Station. They and the detachment then retreated to Sulphur Spring[s] Station, taking the detachment at Bridger's Pass with them. Next morning they started back, commanded by Sergeant McFadden . . . with ten men of Company K, 11th Ohio Volunteer Cavalry. . . . [T]hey are doing all they can to keep open the road, but the force is inadequate to cope with the number of Indians (1865, as quoted in Erb et al. 1989, 45).[7]

St. Mary's Station 🛖 🛻 ▦
Fremont County

Built in 1859 by Russell, Majors, and Waddell as a Pony Express and stage station, St. Mary's Station was located on the upper reach of the Sweetwater River at the eastern base of a sagebrush-covered hillside and was also called Rocky Ridge because it sat just east of that difficult point on the trail. During the Civil War, the station was a garrisoned military post. It also served as a telegraph station. In 1865, Lieutenant Caspar Collins was in charge of this station and others along the Sweetwater River. In a letter to an uncle, he says it was called both Saint Mary's and Rocky Ridge Station. He adds: "Although it is the depot station of the telegraph company, it is not surrounded by a palisade. But it is a place never visited by Indians, hostile or friendly" (Spring 1927, 158–161).

Salt Wells Station
Sweetwater County
This small way station on the Overland Trail was located on Bitter Creek west of Point of Rocks or Rock Point. The site was burned sometime between 1866 and 1868.

Sand Point Trading Post
Platte County
William Guerrier and Seth Ward started the Sand Point Trading Post near Register Cliff on the Oregon Trail in the 1840s. In 1857 they relocated to Fort Laramie where Ward became the post sutler. Sand Point Trading Post, under ownership of Jules Ecoffey, became a Pony Express station from 1860 to 1861 (Goertz 1970), known as Sand Point, Nine Mile, Central Star, or Star Ranch Pony Express Station. This site is also called Ward and Guerrier's Trading Post.

Saratoga Hot Springs
Carbon County
Hot mineral springs bubbled to the surface on both sides of the North Platte River in what is now the town of Saratoga. Although enemy Indian tribes fought each other in the valley area, the hot springs themselves were considered neutral territory, and people from many tribes came to soak in the waters, which they believed had healing powers. The first town developed in the area was known as Warm Springs. In 1884 it was renamed Saratoga for Saratoga Springs, New York. Promoters subsequently developed the mineral springs, bottled and sold the water, and established soaking pools.

The springs are available for public use at the Saratoga Hobo Pool, which is free and open daily, and at the Saratoga Inn Resort.

Sawyers Expedition 🚩 🏴
Crook, Weston, Campbell, Johnson, and Sheridan Counties

Colonel James A. Sawyers (sometimes spelled Sawyer) led a party of civilian surveyors, emigrants, workmen, and a military escort across the Powder River Basin in the summer of 1865 as he identified the route for a wagon road through the region linking the Missouri River and Virginia City, Montana Territory. By following the Niobrara River and then cutting across the Powder River country in present northeastern Wyoming, the Sawyers route was a shorter way for emigrants to reach Virginia City's gold region.

Sawyers Fights, 1865–1866 🏴 ⛰
Sheridan, Johnson, and Campbell Counties

Colonel James A. Sawyers led a military road building crew over the Bozeman Road in the summer of 1865, making improvements to the route across the Powder River Basin.

Near present Gillette, Lakota and Cheyenne Indians attacked the Sawyers expedition, killing three members of the Sawyers party in a number of skirmishes. In two different locations during August 1865—identified as the Bone Pile rifle pits and the Caballo Creek rifle pits (*see individual entries*)—the Sawyers' party circled wagons and dug fortifications for defensive protection.

When they were near Tongue River, the one hundred man road-building crew came under attack by Arapaho Indians on August 31, 1865. As a result of the attacks, three men with Sawyers' command died, including Captain Osmer F. Cole, Sixth Michigan Cavalry, who had ridden ahead of the party as the wagons approached Wolf Creek a couple of miles west of the Tongue River (Badger-Doyle 2001). The harassment by Indians continued for nearly two weeks as the road-building operation moved west. Sawyers subsequently retreated until he had support of soldiers from General P. E. Connor's Powder River expeditionary force.

In 1866 Sawyers returned to the region where Lakota and Cheyenne warriors attacked his party several times. In one incident,

The Seminoe's Fort reproduction is near Devil's Gate. (*Candy Moulton*)

Sawyers' party dug rifle pits northwest of the present T-7 Ranch in Campbell County at a site that has since been obliterated by coal mine activity.

Seminoe's Fort
Natrona County

Archaeologists excavated this trading establishment in 2001, uncovering artifacts from the period of its use in the 1850s, which are now on display at a recreation of the fort. The Church of Jesus Christ of Latter-day Saints built the reproduction of the post known as Seminoe's Fort and sometimes called Devil's Gate Fort for its location near Devil's Gate. Basil Lajuenesse, whose nickname was "Seminoe," built the post before 1855, abandoning it before the fall of 1856. That year when freezing, starving members of the LDS Martin Handcart Company struggled in to the site, they found some of the houses that had been Seminoe's Fort already beginning to deteriorate. They took shelter in portions that remained and burned logs and other combustible materials from the buildings as well. Josiah Rogerson, Sr. was with the Martin Company, and in describing the arrival at Seminoe's Fort in 1856, he writes: "[T]he wagons were banked near the fort. . . . All the people who could crowded into the houses of the fort out of the cold and storm. One crowd cut away the walls of the house they were in for fuel, until half of the roof fell in" (Strong Men, Brave Women 1914, n.p.).

Sherman Hill 🌲 🚂
Laramie and Albany Counties
The highest elevation point on Interstate 80 crosses through the Medicine Bow National Forest between Laramie and Cheyenne over Sherman Hill, a feature named for Union Army General William Tecumseh Sherman. The Union Pacific Railroad pushed across this divide in 1867. Because of the continuing threat from Indian attack as they laid the rail line in this area, railroad workers had constant protection from U. S. military troops based out of Camp Carlin and Fort D. A. Russell.

Short Line Stage Company 🚙
Carbon County
Charles M. Scribner operated this stage company around 1900, serving travelers in the area between Fort Fred Steele or Walcott and Grand Encampment. (*See also* Lake Creek Stage Station.)

Sibley Fight 🏴 ⛺
Sheridan County
On July 7, 1876, Lieutenant F. W. Sibley and thirty men, under orders from General George Crook, headed into the Big Horn Mountains on a scouting expedition. Guided by Baptiste Pourier ("Big Bat") and Frank Grouard, the party was attacked by combined forces of Cheyenne, Arapaho, and Lakota warriors, but it retreated without any casualties. The incident took place near what is now the Sibley Lake Campground in the Bighorn National Forest west of Sheridan (Larson 1978).

Silver Cliff Stage Station 🚙
Niobrara County
Located north of present Lusk, this station on the Cheyenne to Black Hills (Deadwood) stage route was in use from 1876 to 1887.

Simpson's Hollow, Mormon Raid 🏴
Sublette County

On October 5, 1857, Mormon militia, organized by LDS Church President Brigham Young to provide protection for the State of Deseret, where he served as governor, robbed and burned twenty-three supply wagons headed to support the U. S. Army under command of Colonel Albert Sidney Johnston in 1857 at a place that became known as Simpson's Hollow. The site is adjacent to Wyoming Highway 28 about fourteen miles west of Farson. Lot Simpson led the Mormon militia—called the Nauvoo Legion—while Lew Simpson (no relation) was wagon master of the freight wagons owned by Russell, Majors & Waddell under contract to the U. S. Army. The wagons were waiting a military escort because, shortly before the raid, the Mormon militia had attacked a camp of army dragoons (mounted riflemen) near South Pass. Up until that time the army had little inkling that hostilities with the Mormons were imminent, and all army supply trains had been unescorted. The Mormon militia destroyed an estimated 368,000 pounds of freight. The previous day Lot Simpson and his men had burned another group of wagons in an attack near the Big Sandy River.

The loss of supplies slowed Johnston's army, causing it to hold up at the site of a burned-out Fort Bridger later that fall when an early winter storm struck. The troops had short rations throughout the winter. Johnston sent Captain Randolph Marcy overland to Fort Union, New Mexico, for relief supplies, but Marcy did not make it back to the Fort Bridger area until May 1858. (*See also* Utah War of 1857.)

Six Mile Hog Ranch
Goshen County

Named for its distance from Fort Laramie, this hog ranch was in operation perhaps from 1849 until 1889. Here soldiers could find a meal, a drink, and a woman for a romp. The place was so attractive to soldiers that they risked their positions for an opportunity to visit. One soldier went so far as to "steal" an army ambulance to make the trip, subsequently losing ten dollars in pay as well as his stripes. Another soldier served twenty days of hard labor and paid a twelve dollar fine for visiting the Six Mile Hog Ranch without permission (Brown 1995).

The Six Mile Hog Ranch had various owners. Later it became a stage stop on the Cheyenne–Deadwood stage route, where travelers could purchase a meal for fifty cents (Brown 1995).

Sixteen Mile Station 🚃
Carbon County
This station was on the Rawlins to Baggs stage and freight road.

Slade Canyon 🌲
Platte County
Located west of Guernsey, Slade Canyon is named for Joseph Albert "Jack" Slade, a hard man who served as superintendent of the Overland Stage Line operated by Ben Holladay. Slade had an altercation with Jules Beni in Julesburg, Colorado, and eventually killed Beni following another incident, after which he allegedly cut off the man's ears, carrying them in his pocket thereafter. Slade also managed the Horseshoe Station in Platte County and the Virginia Dale Stage Station, which was named for his wife and located in northern Colorado on the Overland Trail, and he worked at Fort Halleck in southern Wyoming. Later he relocated to Virginia City, Montana, where he established a freighting enterprise and also began operating a dairy farm along the Madison River. Slade became a local hero in Montana when he hauled necessary supplies to Virginia City during a drought, but he soon resorted to his earlier mannerisms, arguing or fighting with people, getting drunk, even shooting up the town. Finally he was told to leave town. When he did not, a locally organized vigilance committee, known as the Committee of 100, took Slade into "custody" and took him before the town judge (whom Slade threatened with a concealed gun). Although he was released, ultimately he had pushed the vigilance committee too far, and Slade was hanged in Virginia City on March 10, 1864.

Soldier Creek/Fort/Road/Summit 🌲 🏳 🚂
Carbon County
Troops from Fort Fred Steele established a camp in the Sierra Madre Range south of present Encampment in 1869 to protect men cutting ties for construction of the Union Pacific Railroad. The soldiers' camp

was located near the Encampment River at the mouth of a creek that subsequently became known as Soldier Creek, off Road 550 in the Medicine Bow–Routt National Forest west of Encampment. The road used to reach the camp became known as Soldier's Road, and the tie cutting took place in the area subsequently called Soldier Summit. To protect the road, the soldiers built a small fort of two block houses with a stone fence. The fort, which faced east toward the Encampment River, was just about three-quarters of a mile upstream from the present town of Riverside. At least one documented Indian attack involved soldiers from the fort. About sixty cavalry troops were attacked by Indians of an unknown tribe (although possibly they were Utes who frequented the area) as the soldiers followed the road west of the fort toward the tie camp area. Other troops heard the firing and came to the aid of the soldiers who were under attack. Apparently six Indians died in the battle. There is no report of any other injuries (Peryam 1952).

South Bend Stage Station 🪧 🚃
Sweetwater County
Used by the Pony Express in 1860, this adobe structure was located in what is now the town of Granger. In 1860 Sir Richard Burton said the station was a shanty constructed of stones piled on top of each other, and he notes that the conditions were "a disgrace" making note of "the squalor and filth. . . . the flies—unequivocal sign of unclean living!—darkened the table and covered everything put upon it" (Burton 1860, as quoted in Haines 1981, 261) (*See* Pony Express Trail.)

South Bend Station 🚃
Sweetwater County
Also called Ham's Fork Station, this station was on the Overland Trail. (*See* Overland Trail.)

South Pass 🪧 🌲 🚃
Fremont County
South Pass, a sagebrush-covered pass that marks the Continental Divide, is the reason more than 400,000 emigrants on their way to

This marker on South Pass notes the crossing in 1836 of missionary wives Narcissa Prentiss Whitman and Eliza Hart Spalding. (*Candy Moulton*)

Oregon, California, or Utah crossed through central Wyoming between 1841 and 1869. Indian and game trails crossed the pass long before Robert Stuart and his six companions saw it in 1812 (*see* Astorian Camp). Stuart did not know his exact location, and he and his party did not actually cross the pass itself, but he reported on it when he returned to St. Louis from Astoria. In 1824 Thomas Fitzpatrick, traveling with the Rocky Mountain Fur Company and companions Jedediah Smith and William Sublette, relocated the pass. Captain Benjamin L. E. Bonneville took wagons over it in 1832, and after missionary wives Narcissa Whitman and Eliza Spalding crossed the pass in 1835 in a light wagon and sometimes riding sidesaddle on their horses, it became clear it could become the main route to the Pacific Northwest country, which became known as Oregon.

The pass is on public land accessible off Wyoming Highway 28 midway between Farson and Lander.

South Pass City 🚏
Fremont County
Gold discoveries led to establishment of South Pass City in 1867. Within a year the community had 3,000 residents living in town or nearby. It quickly became a center of political clout. E. G. Nickerson and William Bright, candidates for the position as Representative to the Wyoming Territorial Legislature, heard appeals from Esther Hobart Morris, and possibly others, to introduce legislation that would give women suffrage. Bright ultimately won the election and sponsored the bill that gave Wyoming women the right to vote in 1869, the first state in the nation to grant woman suffrage. The legislature also provided other opportunities for women to serve on juries and in the court. Morris in 1870 became the first female justice of the peace in the United States when she was appointed to the position to replace J. W. Stillman. While Wyoming first approved a bill that would allow women to vote, the first women in the nation to cast ballots were from Utah, a state that also granted suffrage and allowed women to participate at the polls just weeks before the Wyoming women actually marked their first ballots.

Original buildings from South Pass City have been restored at the site that is now a Wyoming State Historic Site located west of Lander off Wyoming Highway 28.

South Pass Station 🚌 🏳
Fremont County
Another name for Burnt Ranch (*see entry*) or Upper Sweetwater Station, this station was used by the Pony Express in 1860 and 1861. After completion of the transcontinental telegraph in 1861, South Pass Station served as a telegraph station, with a military command on hand to provide protection and maintain the telegraph line.

Split Rock 🚩 🌲 🛞
Natrona County

A natural break in the rocky range of the Rattlesnake Mountains east of the Sweetwater River, Split Rock became a landmark for travelers on the Oregon, Mormon, and California Trails. Split Rock is about ten miles south of Jeffrey City. Two different roadside pullouts along U.S. 287 offer a view of the landmark.

Split Rock Station 🚩 🛞 🏴
Natrona County

In 1859, William Russell, Alexander Majors, and William Waddell built the Split Rock Station near the rock landmark of the same name, about ten miles south of present Jeffrey City. It served their freight, stage, and mail route and was a Pony Express station in 1860 and 1861. It was also a telegraph station and a garrisoned military post.

Traveling toward Fort Bridger in 1857 with Colonel Albert Sidney Johnston, William A. Carter writes:

> It was not until near sunset before we came in sight of the Troops encamped in the Valley on the right of the road and on the opposite side of the river . . . soon [we] were seated around a brilliant fire and enjoying ourselves at seeing the grass extending far up the sides of the huge piles of rock that hung far above our heads, covered here and there by the dark cedar. The Picture was worthy the pencil of the artist. Our camp was near what is called the split in the rock, a remarkable cleft in the top of the mountain which can be seen at a great distance from either direction (Wyoming Recreation Commission 1988, 176).

On July 30, 1862, Henry R. Herr notes in his diary:

> Camped at Split Rock, where there is quartered 50 soldiers for protection of the emigrants, 200 wagons passed today on their way to Salmon River [Idaho] mines. Soldiers composed of 6th Ohio Reg (quoted in Haines 1981, 215).

The Indians were becoming concerned by the number of emigrants and other travelers passing across their lands, affecting grazing opportunities for wild game and making it more difficult for the tribes to find food. In July 1862, traditionally friendly Shoshone Indians and their Bannock allies attacked stage stations along the Sweetwater River and on west to Bear River Valley in present Idaho, cutting telegraph lines and capturing livestock needed for the stage operations.

Spring Creek Raid
Washakie County

Joe Emge and Joe Allemand moved sheep into the Bighorn Basin near Tensleep in 1909, turning them loose on range along Spring Creek. Cattlemen adamantly opposed the importation of sheep. The night of April 2, raiders visited the camp where Emge and Allemand headquartered their sheep herd, killing the animals and the owners. The National Wool Growers' Association immediately posted a reward of $20,000 for the "Ten Sleep Raiders." Soon a grand jury convened. Eventually seven men were arrested on charges related to the raid. Two cut deals to testify against their cohorts, and tensions rose to fever pitch, forcing local authorities to call on assistance from federal troops who responded to the area to maintain order.

Eventually the five accused men were found guilty and sentenced to prison for terms ranging from three years to life. An interpretive marker has been placed near the site of the raid south of Tensleep along Highway 434.

Spring Ranch Station
Goshen County

This is another name for the Cold Springs Pony Express Station. (*See* Pony Express Trail.)

Spring Station
Uinta County

This Pony Express relay station was also known as Aspen Station and Quaking Asp Springs Station. (*See* Pony Express Trail.)

Squaw Mountain ♣ ⛺

Carbon County

This mountain on the west side of the Sierra Madre Range and east of Savery gets its name from an attack by Indians on trappers in August 1841. During the fight, the Arapaho, Cheyenne, and Lakota warriors sent the women with them to the mountain for safety. (*See* Little Snake River, Indian Attack.)

Stansbury Expedition, 1850 🛶 🚛

Laramie, Albany, Carbon, Sweetwater, and Uinta Counties

Captain Howard Stansbury, with guide Jim Bridger, led this Corps of Topographical Engineers expedition in 1850. He recognized the potential for a shorter route to the West than the Oregon Trail, and the route Stansbury traveled, when connected to the Lodgepole Trail in western Nebraska, became the Overland Trail (*see entry*).

Stuart Campsite 🍴 🚛

Goshen County

In 1812 Robert Stuart and six companions spent part of the winter in a small shack they constructed at a site east of present Torrington and near the present Wyoming–Nebraska border as they traveled east from Fort Astoria, Oregon, to St. Louis (*see also* Astorian Camp).

Sublette Cutoff, California Trail 🚛

Sublette and Lincoln Counties

Originally pioneered by Caleb Greenwood and called the Greenwood Cutoff (*see entry*), this route served as a shortcut for travelers on their way to California's gold fields. The route split from the California Trail at Parting of the Ways. It passed north of present Farson and then continued west to the Green River before following a route generally along Wyoming Highways 372 and U.S. 189 to Farson. The route crossed the Tunp Range and the Ham's Fork of the Green River south of Commissary Ridge, and then it departed from Wyoming near present Cokeville. Other shortcuts also were established in that same general region, including the Dempsey–Hockaday Cutoff, the Kinney Cutoff, and the Slate Creek Cutoff.

This building, now on a private ranch in Carbon County, served the Overland Trail era as Sulphur Springs Station. (*Candy Moulton*)

Sulphur Springs Station 🚃 🏴
Carbon County

This stage station on the Overland Trail also served the Rawlins to Baggs freight and stage road. It was built in early July 1862 for use by the military and as a home station on the Overland Stage Company mail route operated by Ben Holladay. It also served as an important telegraph station due to its location on both the Overland Trail and on the route between Rawlins and Baggs.

The station, located at the western end of Muddy Creek Canyon, served as headquarters for the Eleventh Kansas Volunteers, commanded by Major R. A. Morse. The soldiers dug lookout positions on the hill above the station and constructed a tunnel from the water spring to the top of one of the pits. The station had a toll bridge in operation over Muddy Creek (with a charge of 50 cents per team), an "elephant corral" for covered wagons, and a blacksmith shop, a hay shed, an ice house, an arsenal, and a root cellar.

Traveling the trail in 1863 with the Joseph Hooper wagon train, Howard Cutting writes:

> We were allowed the privilege of crossing the creek on a bridge for twenty-five cents a wagon, or by fording for nothing. Most of us took the Free Ticket. The ford was very bad, the bank being very steep, in fact straight down for near four foot, had undoubtedly been cut down purposely by the bridge owners (Alcorn 1984, 44).

In August 1863 Sioux and Cheyenne Indians attacked a wagon train near Sulphur Springs Station, killing twenty-nine men, women, and children. Even more lives might have been lost had not soldiers commanded by Major R. A. Morse learned of the attack and ridden to the defense of the overland travelers. An estimated ninety Indians died in the fighting (Barnhart 1969; Hafen 1926; Rosenberg 1989). (*See also* Muddy Creek Massacre.)

Sun Ranch

Natrona and Carbon Counties

Founded in 1872, this ranch was carved out along the Sweetwater River by a man who helped teach William F. "Buffalo Bill" Cody how to shoot: Thomas de Beau Soleil, better known as Tom Sun. The Oregon, California, and Mormon trails crossed the ranch, as did the Pony Express route and the transcontinental telegraph. Devil's Gate, a natural landmark through which the Sweetwater River flows, served as a backdrop for the main ranch buildings. The headquarters of the ranch remained in family ownership until 1996 when the Sun family sold to the Church of Jesus Christ of Latter-day Saints, which considers Martin's Cove, an area near the ranch headquarters, as sacred ground due to the deaths of handcart emigrants in 1856. (*See also* Martin's Cove.)

Sweetwater River

Natrona, Carbon, and Fremont Counties

In 1823 fur trader William Ashley named this central Wyoming stream the Sweetwater River when trappers told him the water had a sweet taste. Legend says a pack animal carrying sugar fell in the water, giving it that sweetness. Certainly emigrants traveling west on the Oregon, California, and Mormon trails found the water cold and clean compared with the often muddy streams they had followed over much of the route from the East.

Sweetwater Station 🚃 🏴

Natrona County

In 1860 and 1861, a crude log shack served as a Pony Express relay station and became known as Sweetwater Station. Located near Independence Rock, midway between Rawlins and Casper adjacent to Wyoming Highway 220, it had a horse shed but no corral. During the Civil War, the facility was upgraded as a military post with a single company garrisoned at the post at any one time to protect the overland travel routes and the transcontinental telegraph line. In a letter to his mother July 16, Lieutenant Caspar Collins, who commanded the post in 1862 and was later killed in a fight near Platte Bridge Station, writes:

> This is the worst country for winds I ever saw. Yesterday . . . it commenced to blow and it is blowing yet. . . . Major [Jim] Bridger went off this morning up into the mountains to get out of the wind. He said he is going to get in some canon and make a large fire (Spring 1927, 116).[8]

From his post at Sweetwater Station, Lieutenant Collins commanded troops protecting four stations along the Oregon Trail route, which were also in use as telegraph stations. Writing from Fort Laramie to an uncle on December 13, 1864, he says:

> I am now stationed on Sweetwater River, a tributary of the Platte. I have four block stations under my charge. The first is Sweetwater Bridge, the bridge by which the emigrants cross the river on their way to California and Oregon; the second is Three Crossings of Sweetwater; the third, Rocky Ridge; and the fourth is South Pass. I make my headquarters at the first. . . .
> From my station to the upper one, it is one hundred and four miles, and I have to ride it and back about every two

weeks, so it keeps me pretty busy. We have plenty of game up there by riding about 20 or 25 miles for it. There are buffalo, elk, mountain sheep, black-tailed deer and antelope. There is plenty of antelope close by the station, but they have lived so much on sage brush that they taste of it. . . .

The post was built by Co. D and intended as quarters for forty men. But I have only twenty there now. It is situated on a hill about 50 yards from the Sweetwater River and overlooking the bridge. The second assistant surgeon of the regiment is stationed with me (Carley 1954, 75–76).

Texas Cattle Trail 🚏
Laramie, Platte, Goshen, Niobrara, Converse, Weston, Crook, Campbell, Johnson, and Sheridan Counties

Cattle from Texas came north in 1866 over a route through New Mexico and Colorado that became known as the Goodnight–Loving Trail, named for the two men who forged the route: Charles Goodnight and Oliver Loving. They sold their herd to John Wesley Iliff, a man who became a major cattleman with headquarters in present northeastern Colorado centered by the town of Iliff that he helped establish. Once Iliff bought the Goodnight–Loving cattle herd in 1866, he pushed the animals on to range even farther north into what is present Wyoming. The Texas Cattle Trail that made its first incursion into Wyoming near Cheyenne ultimately extended to the west and north across eastern Wyoming and eventually on into present Montana.

The Texas Cattle Trail passed near the present communities of Pine Bluffs, Cheyenne, Chugwater, Lusk, Moorcroft, and Sheridan. Markers indicate the trail near Lusk on U.S. 18/20, along Highway 387 west of Wright, and in Moorcroft.

Three Crossings Stage Station 🚙 🏴 ⛺
Fremont County

This stage station located about five miles east of present Jeffrey City predated the Three Crossings military station located about a mile to the northeast, and it was in a more defensible position during the period of Indian unrest along the Sweetwater River in the 1860s.

Sir Richard Burton reached this station in 1860 and writes that it was "neatly swept and garnished, papered and ornamented. . . . The table-cloth was clean, so was the cooking, so were the children" (1862, 154–155). Three Crossings served as a home station for the Pony Express, and William F. Cody lived there when he rode for that service.

The original station may have been built of logs, but information Lester Bagley provided during the Oregon Trail Trek No. Five, conducted in 1957 by the Wyoming State Historical Society, indicates the following:

> [D]uring the stage coach period, the Three Crossing Station was rebuilt of stone and logs. The main part of the building was a large stone structure which was flanked by log houses and surrounded by a stockade to the south. A lookout was erected on the northwest corner (Carley 1957b, 191).

In July 1861, Three Crossings Station became a U. S. Post Office, and the following year Shoshone and Bannock Indians attacked a mail party of nine men and two coaches as they approached the station. T. S. Boardman was with the party and later recounted the incident:

> We drove to the top of a slight elevation to the left of the road; the other coach was driven up along side, distant about ten feet; mules badly frightened; one of them was shot through the mouth, and the bullets whistling rapidly among them it was thought best to let them go. They were accordingly cut loose and were soon driven up a canon to the southwest on the road, by some ten or twelve Indians. Everything that could afford protection, mail sacks, blankets, buffalo robes, etc., were thrown out of the coaches, against the wheels and along the east side of us, behind which we barricaded ourselves. James Brown who was standing by the hind wheel of one of the coaches, then received a shot in the left side of the face . . . Lem Flowers [Division Agent] was then struck in the hip . . . Phil Rogers received two arrows in the right shoulder . . . James Anderson was shot through the left

leg, and William Reed through the small of the back (Carley 1957b, 190–191).

When the Indians withdrew, the mail party made its way to Three Crossings Station. There the mail party members found the station agent, his wife and three children, and men employed by the stage company, though Indians had raided the station and taken all the mules and eight head of cattle. "Here the station house and stable were made into a fort," Boardman writes (Carley 1957b, 191).

Lieutenant Colonel William O. Collins was at Three Crossings Station in 1862 along with his son, Lieutenant Caspar Collins, who writes about the stations in the Sweetwater country, including Three Crossings, St. Mary's (or Rocky Ridge), and South Pass (or Upper Crossings):

> These were "home stations," bigger than others along the way, and included a building where stage passengers could find food and lodging, a telegraph office, a corral, and a barn to house supplies and hay. All were much in need of repair, another job for the Ohioans stationed there. Over the summer the troops also built barracks and stables (1862, as quoted in Jones 2005, 76).

Three Crossings Station, Civil War Era 🏴
Fremont County

Located just more than a mile from the earlier Three Crossings Station, this military post was fortified and garrisoned by a single company of soldiers. It served as a telegraph station but probably did not serve any stagecoach traffic because most of that service shifted away from the Oregon–California route through the Sweetwater Valley and moved south to the Overland Trail route where there was believed to be less likelihood of Indian attack. As a result of hostilities in this area, fourteen soldiers were buried near the station. In 1928 officials removed and re-interred thirteen of the bodies, leaving only the grave of Bennett Tribbett, Company B, Eleventh Ohio.

In July 1862, troops from Company D, Eleventh Ohio Cavalry, rode to Sweetwater Station under command of Major John O'Ferrall (a physician who served under Lieutenant Caspar Collins), who "met much of Company A and employees of the Overland Mail Company with their coaches and stock, and escorted them south to the new mail route" then established on the Overland Trail across southern Wyoming. Almost as soon as they departed from the station, Indians attacked and burned it (Jones 2005, 86–87).

Lieutenant Collins, who first spent time at Three Crossings in 1862 with his father, Lieutenant Colonel William O. Collins, commander of the Eleventh Ohio Cavalry, notes in a letter to his uncle that the station was "surrounded by a palisade, varying from 12 to 15 feet high, and surmounted by a large lookout and block house that sweeps the surrounding country" (Spring 1927, 89; Carley 1957a, 76).

Three Mile Hog Ranch
Goshen County
Also called the Fort Laramie Hog Ranch, this establishment constructed by Jules Ecoffey and Adolph Cuny in 1872, did not raise pigs. Located three miles from Fort Laramie, the hog ranch instead was a place for soldiers to relax by playing cards or billiards, having a fifty-cent meal, or visiting the girls whom Teamster Harry Young called "a very low, tough set." Lieutenant John G. Bourke in 1877 concurred, noting they were "as hardened and depraved a set of witches as could be found on the face of the globe" (Wyoming Recreation Commission 1988, 98).

The ranch had many buildings, including a store, blacksmith shop, bunkhouse, billiard hall and saloon, warehouse, ice house, large corral, and six two-room cottages where the "working" girls lived and did business.

Three Mile started as a trading post but expanded to bolster business and trade opportunities. Ownership of the ranch changed from Cuny and Ecoffey to a man named Bottlejohn and then it sold to John Thornmahley & Company, which offered hay and feed for a short time. Other owners and managers included Hank Steward, Andy Ryan, Bob Osborne, Johnny Owens, and Henry Riterling.

Tie Siding
Albany County
Railroad workers established this community in 1868 as they cut ties needed for construction of the Union Pacific Railroad. It later became

a supply center for ranches and in 2010 still has a small store that sells antiques and second-hand items. It is located seventeen miles south of Laramie on U. S. Highway 287.

Tongue River, Battle of 〒 🏴 𝘼
Sheridan County

The Battle of Tongue River took place August 28, 1865, as part of the Connor Expedition. This incident is also known as the Connor Battle (*see entry*). The site is a park and Wyoming State Historic Site in the town of Ranchester.

Torrington Station 🚂
Goshen County

This Pony Express station was also known as Spring Ranch and Cold Springs Station. (*See* Pony Express Trail.)

Transcontinental Telegraph Stations
Platte, Natrona, Fremont, Carbon, Sweetwater, and Uinta Counties

To protect the transcontinental telegraph after its completion in 1861, the U. S. Army established stations where troops could live and be in a position to respond quickly to any threats or breaks in the line. The stations, from east to west, were located at Horseshoe Creek, LaBonte (Camp Marshall), LaPrele, Deer Creek, Platte Bridge (Fort Caspar), Sweetwater, St. Mary's, and Burnt Ranch (South Pass) (*see individual entries*).

Tri-Territory Site 🌲
Sweetwater County

The Tri-Territory Site, located on U. S. Bureau of Land Management land in a remote area northeast of Rock Springs, marks the location of the Forty-second Parallel, which once divided the American West into possessions held by Spain, Great Britain, and France. The United States obtained the French Territory to the north and east in the Louisiana Purchase of 1803. The northwest portion that once belonged to Great Britain became Oregon Territory in August 1848, while the Spanish holdings were ceded to the United States in the Mexican Treaty of Guadalupe Hildago in January 1848.

Twenty Mile Station 🚌
Carbon County
This station was on the Rawlins to Baggs stage and freight road.

Union Pacific Railroad 🚂
Laramie, Albany, Carbon, Sweetwater, and Uinta Counties
In 1867 the Union Pacific Railway Company began laying the steel tracks that would link the nation when it reached Promontory, Utah, and the lines of the Central Pacific Railway. The railroad work gangs swung into what would become Cheyenne during July, establishing the first of many end-of-tracks, or hell-on-wheels, towns as they pushed westward. Those rail towns with the names Carbon, Benton, Rawlins Spring, Tipton, Point of Rocks, Green River, Bear River City, and Evanston grew quickly, and many of them died just as suddenly. By the time the railroad was completed across Wyoming in late 1868 and linked with the Central Pacific in May 1869, communities such as Benton and Tipton had already pretty much disappeared. Other towns survived and became the first county seats for the five original counties in Wyoming: Laramie County, (with Cheyenne as the county seat); Albany County (Laramie); Carbon County (Rawlins); Sweetwater County (Green River); and Uinta County (Evanston).

Many government incentives aided the railroad construction, including a grant of land for alternating sections twenty miles south and twenty miles north of the line all along the route across Wyoming. As a result of this land grant, the Union Pacific Railway Company had about 12 million acres of land it could sell to generate revenue. While such sales were common in eastern Wyoming and Nebraska, the land west of Laramie was more arid and therefore less desirable, so the UP retained much of that land grant, creating a checkerboard of public and private lands that still exists in Wyoming.

Although the surface value of the land did not entice homesteaders, minerals underlying the region in western Wyoming benefited the railway company. The Union Pacific knew of coal resources along the route even before beginning construction and began mining

The Union Pacific laid tracks across Wyoming in 1868. (*Courtesy Wyoming State Archives*)

operations in 1868 at Carbon soon following suit near Rock Springs (*see indiviudual entries*).

The railroad construction also involved a governmental subsidy to the UP under the Pacific Railroad Act of May 1862. For much of the route, the company received $16,000 per mile, but that figure rose to $48,000 per mile west of Cheyenne due to the more difficult terrain over the next a 150-mile stretch. After the track crossed that area, the payment dropped to $32,000 per mile to the point in Utah where the Union Pacific track connected with line laid by workers for the Central Pacific (Moulton 1995, 212–216).

Upper Sweetwater Station
Fremont County
This is another name for Burnt Ranch (*see entry*).

Utah War of 1857
Sweetwater and Uinta Counties
When President James Buchanan assumed office in 1857, he took steps to replace Utah governor Brigham Young, who was perceived as being too powerful in the territory because he served dual roles as governor and president of the Church of Jesus Christ of Latter-day Saints. There was opposition to the move from within Utah so Buchanan ordered a military escort that would eventually install the

new governor. Troops began marching toward Utah even before Buchanan appointed Alfred Cumming as the new governor. When Young learned of the army's march toward Utah, he organized militia units to defend the settlements. At that time the Mormons controlled Fort Bridger. Young subsequently posted units in present southwest Wyoming to slow the advance of the oncoming army. The initial commander of the U. S. Army troops was Colonel E. B. Alexander, who established a camp on the Ham's Fork of the Green River that became known as Camp Scott. Mormon parties began harassing the troops there, eventually destroying freight wagons en route to the army troops with supplies at Simpson's Hollow (*see entry*).

In late August, Alexander was replaced by Colonel Albert Sidney Johnston, breveted as general to command the Utah Expedition, whose arrival at Camp Scott was delayed. Eventually the troops marched beyond Camp Scott to the ruins of Fort Bridger and Fort Supply, which the Mormons had burned as they retreated toward Utah to eliminate availability of resources for military use. Johnston's army subsequently established a winter camp at Fort Bridger, but they had only limited supplies, so Johnston ordered a relief party to Fort Union in New Mexico. Captain Randolph B. Marcy led that party through Colorado, where no forts had been established west of the Continental Divide, in a harrowing crossing that the men barely survived. At Fort Union, Marcy put together relief supplies. He then followed the Trappers Trail and Cherokee Trail north through present Colorado and took the Cherokee route west across present southern Wyoming to Fort Bridger, arriving in the spring of 1858.

Johnston's army did march on in to Salt Lake City in the spring of 1858, and in spite of the previous year's preparations when Mormon militia developed defensive positions along the route, no resistance came from the Mormons as the army entered the city and installed the new governor.

Ute Indian Attack, 1870s Δ
Carbon County

Ute Indians killed Joe Brun, Frank Marrion, and John Scott, known as "Old Man Scott," at a site about five miles east of the present town of Encampment along the Cherokee Trail in the early 1870s.

John H. Mullison and Tom Castle found the mutilated bodies of the three men and buried them in a common grave. They then took a large rock and carved on it "Three white men killed by Indians." The original rock is now at the Grand Encampment Museum and a replacement has been set at the site of the burial, which is on private land.

Ute Indian Incursions of 1879 🛆
Carbon County

During the summer of 1879, Ute Indians left the White River Reservation in northwest Colorado to hunt in southern Wyoming. At the time only a few ranches were scattered in the upper North Platte River Valley area in the region around today's Encampment and Saratoga. Because of the tension between the Utes and their agent, Nathan C. Meeker, ranchers were on heightened alert that summer. Several of them contacted military authorities stationed at Fort Fred Steele, such as rancher William Brauer, who wrote to Major Thomas Tipton Thornburgh in July concerning Utes who had been in the area: "I hear of no acts of hostility, and, in fact, I know that none was committed, as I have seen nearly all the ranchmen in 100 miles of us since [the Utes'] departure" (Alcorn 1984, 101).

In September Meeker's anxiety level reached its apex, and he requested that troops from Fort Fred Steele come to the White River Agency. At the time, Major Thornburgh was fishing at Battle Lake in the Sierra Madres. A Private O'Malley located Thornburgh at his fishing camp and later accompanied Thornburgh and other troops as they rode from Fort Fred Steele toward the agency. The troops ran into a Ute ambush on Milk Creek, in Colorado. The Utes killed Thornburgh and other soldiers before they surrounded the remaining troops. Joe Rankin and three other men broke through the Ute lines to ride for help, and Rankin eventually reached Rawlins where he notified military officials of the attack on Thornburgh's troops. A relief party was quickly organized at Fort D.A. Russell and rushed by train to Rawlins then overland along the Rawlins to Baggs road to the Milk Creek battle site. The Utes withdrew when the additional soldiers reached the besieged troops.

Throughout those last days of September and early October, ranch families in Carbon County remained on high alert. Many of them congregated in Warm Springs [Saratoga]. In the area of Swan, about one mile downstream from the present town of Riverside, ranchers gathered at the home of Guy Nichols for mutual protection. In spite of the high tension, no Ute attacks occurred in Carbon County during the period. (*See also* Fort Fred Steele.)

Vore Buffalo Jump 🌲 🛖
Crook County
The Vore Buffalo Jump, named for the ranching family that owned the property in the late twentieth century, was in use perhaps centuries earlier by indigenous people who hazed buffalo through the valley so they would fall into the deep cavern. The use of buffalo jumps for harvesting animals for meat and hides was common among Plains Indian tribes before the arrival of horses, which were brought to the American West by Spanish explorers in the 1500s and obtained by Shoshone and Comanche Indians during the 1700s then later traded to other tribes. The Vore Buffalo Jump is adjacent to Interstate 90 some ten miles east of Sundance.

Wagon Box Fight 🏳️ 🏴 🛖
Sheridan and Johnson Counties
Woodcutters from Fort Phil Kearny took refuge behind a barricade of wagon boxes on August 2, 1867, as Lakota warriors led by Red Cloud attacked them in what became the Wagon Box Fight.

Led by Major James Powell, the woodcutting guard comprised fifty-one men from Fort Phil Kearny when they began their work on July 31, 1868. As the woodcutters spread out with two primary camps located about a mile apart near Piney Creek, Powell divided his command. On the morning of August 2, a large band of Lakota warriors attacked the stock tenders and woodcutters, forcing them to flee toward Fort Phil Kearny. The attack was so sudden that twenty-eight soldiers and civilian woodcutters could not retreat and had to crouch behind the wagon boxes as the Indians peppered them with arrows and rifle fire. The troops held off the larger force of Indians because the soldiers commanded the high ground and they also had superior equipment. The troopers had recently been issued breech-loading Springfield rifles plus around one thousand rounds of ammunition.

The Indians expected a delay after the first round of shots by the soldiers so they continued toward the wagon box enclosure only to be struck with additional rounds because the troops no longer had to reload their rifles after each shot.

Although they suffered from lack of water, the troops held the Indians at bay until the afternoon when reinforcement troops rode in from the fort, a few miles downstream along Piney Creek. The besieged soldiers had prepared to kill themselves if the Indians overran their position. Private Sam Gibson later said they attached shoe laces to the triggers of their rifles, preparing to hold the strings between their toes to commit suicide if necessary (Moulton 1995, 317).

Three soldiers died in the attack and possibly fifty or sixty Indians. The battle site, located about a mile west of Story, is now owned by the Fort Phil Kearny/Bozeman Trail Association.

Ward and Guerrier's Trading Post
Platte County
See Sand Point Trading Post.

Washakie Grave
Fremont County
One of the most influential Shoshones ever, Chief Washakie guided his people for many decades, generally taking the stand that peace was preferable to war. As a result, the Shoshones caused few problems for overland emigrants, though they did later raid some military posts and stage stations in their territory. Washakie, who had been a chief or sub-chief from 1830, died on the Wind River Reservation on February 22, 1900. After his death, Camp Brown Commander Clough Overton issued General Order No. 2:

> Washakie was of commanding presence. . . . His countenance was one of rugged strength mingled with kindness. His military service is an unbroken record for gallantry, and officers now wearing a star fought with him in their subaltern days. The respect and friendship of these former commanders was prized to the day of his death. Washakie was a great man, for he was a brave man and a good man. The

Like most of the stations along the Overland Trail, the Washakie Station walls were constructed of rough sandstone blocks. (*Candy Moulton*)

spirit of his loyalty and courage will speak to soldiers; the memory of his love for his own people will linger to assist them in their troubles, and he will never be forgotten so long as the mountains and streams of Wyoming, which were his home, bear his name.

The Post Commander directs that Washakie be buried with military honors in the Post Cemetery at 2:00 p.m. tomorrow (WY Recreation Commission 1988, 92).

Washakie's burial was in the Old Military Cemetery at Camp Brown on the Wind River Reservation west of Fort Washakie, where the grave remains and can be visited by the public.

Washakie Station
Carbon County

Unlike some stations located nearer to the timbered slopes of the Sierra Madre and Medicine Bow mountain ranges and therefore made of logs, this station on the Overland Trail was constructed of

Two graves rest on the hill above the Washakie Station on the Overland Trail in Carbon County. (*Candy Moulton*)

native sandstone rocks stacked on top of each other and held together with mortar made from clay and sand. The structures had pole roofs covered with dirt as well as dirt floors. Named for Shoshone Chief

Washakie, this station is on public land southwest of Rawlins approximately three and a half miles west of the Overland Trail marker on Wyoming Highway 789 between Baggs and Creston Junction. Some sources refer to it as the Waskie Station (Carley 1961b).

Washburn, Langford, Doane Expedition Campsite 🛶
Yellowstone National Park
One of the first official exploratory expeditions in Yellowstone National Park took place in 1870 under the direction of General Henry D. Washburn, surveyor general for public lands in Montana Territory. He was accompanied by Nathaniel P. Langford and Lieutenant Gustavius C. Doane, commander of the expedition's military escort. The party camped in present Yellowstone National Park where the Firehole and Gibbon Rivers merge to form the Madison River.

Whiskey Gap 🏴
Carbon County
This site gets its name from an incident in 1862 when Major John O'Ferrall of Company A, Sixth Ohio Cavalry (later to become the Eleventh Ohio), traveled from Devil's Gate to near Elk Mountain to establish Fort Halleck. After a first day of travel, the party stopped in a gap where there was a spring and wood for fires. According to Historian C. G. Coutant, not long after making camp, Major O'Ferrall found that some of the men had been drinking. He ordered a search of the military wagons and those of the emigrants traveling with them. When Lieutenant W. H. Brown conducted the search, he found a barrel of whiskey in one wagon. It was removed and destroyed, but the contents ran into the spring. That, Coutant reports, caused the soldiers to rush "forward with cups, canteens and camp kettles to save what they could of the whiskey" (Erb et al. 1989, 51).

Wilcox Station 🚂
Albany County
Located about six miles from Rock Creek and near the town of Rock River, the Wilcox Station on the Union Pacific was near the site of a daring train robbery June 2, 1899. Robbers boarded the westbound train near Wilcox, ordering the engineer to continue west until the

train had crossed the bridge. Then, knowing that troops were on another oncoming westbound train, the bandits and their accomplices blew up the Wilcox Bridge before using some dynamite on the safe in the train they had commandeered. Once they had broken into the safe, the thieves took their loot, approximately $60,000, and rode out of the country. Some of them likely headed north toward Hole-in-the-Wall while others holed up near Elk Mountain.

It's not certain who was a part of the robber party, but those believed to be involved were "Flat Nose" George Currie, Harvey Logan, Lonnie Logan, and Bob Lee. There has always been speculation that Butch Cassidy was involved in at least planning the Wilcox robbery, but there is no concrete evidence that he was present at the time. Wild Bunch researcher and Sundance Kid biographer Donna Ernst believes that Sundance (Harry Longabaugh) was involved at Wilcox. Elzy Lay, another Wild Bunch member, also may have been involved in the Wilcox robbery (Patterson 1998).

Willow Springs Station
Albany County
This stage station on the Overland Trail was located fifteen miles north of Virginia Dale Station and the Wyoming–Colorado border. The station got its name for its location in a willow grove that also had a spring.

Willow Springs Station (Ryan Hill)
Natrona County
This campsite on the Oregon–California Trail served stage traffic during the 1860s. Sir Richard Burton notes it was a "little doggery boasting of a shed and a bunk, but no corral. . . . The water was unusually good at Willow Springs; unfortunately there was nothing else" (Burton 1862; reprint 1990, 147). This site was at the foot of Ryan Hill. (*See also* Prospect Hill.)

Willows Station
Carbon County
This station was on the Rawlins to Baggs stage and freight road.

Wind River Indian Reservation 🛆
Fremont County

The July 3, 1868, Treaty of Fort Bridger established the Shoshone and Bannock Indian Reservation, better known as the Wind River Reservation. Initially the reservation included land from the Wind River Valley, and it extended to the west and south as far as Fort Bridger. The size was later reduced.

The reservation set aside for the Shoshone Indians under Chief Washakie was opened with Shoshone permission in 1877 for their traditional enemies the Arapahos. Already reduced in size by then, the reservation boundary was further scaled back in 1904 when the Shoshones ceded land to the north in an agreement that turned the hot mineral springs in Thermopolis over to state officials in what became known as the Gift of the Waters. The reservation itself encompasses much of the Wind River Basin, skirting to or encompassing the communities of Lander, Hudson, Riverton, Pavillion, Ethete, Fort Washakie, and Crowheart.

Each tribe maintains its own leadership and cultural traditions with the Shoshones generally living in the western portion of the reservation with headquarters at Fort Washakie and the Arapahos to the east with headquarters at Ethete.

Wyoming Territorial Prison 🚏
Albany County

Before Laramie was a formal community, it was an end-of-tracks, or hell-on-wheels, town of Union Pacific Railroad construction workers and as such had more than a few residents who created trouble. Early lawbreakers were thrown in the brig at Fort Sanders, but as the town grew, it became apparent the area needed a bigger and better place to house criminals. Workers began constructing the Wyoming Territorial Prison and completed the facility near the banks of the Laramie River on October 15, 1872. The following year fire damaged the prison, but it was quickly rebuilt. It served as both a state and federal penal institution from 1872 until 1902 when a new prison was built in Rawlins. The last prisoners held at the Wyoming Territorial Prison in Laramie were transferred to Rawlins in 1903, and the early prison was put into use as a livestock experimental farm for the University of Wyoming. That use discontinued in the 1970s when a new UW livestock farm was established just outside the city. The old prison then underwent a major restoration project and reopened as the Wyoming Territorial Park to give visitors an opportunity to tour a territorial prison.

Yellowstone Expedition, 1886–1887 🛶
Yellowstone National Park

Arctic explorer Lieutenant Frederick Schwatka led a winter expedition through Yellowstone National Park in 1886–1887. The explorers used Norwegian skis and Canadian-style web snowshoes as they traveled through the park, carrying scientific and photographic equipment to gather information about the park in winter. Although Lieutenant Schwatka became ill and abandoned the expedition, four of the men continued. They included photographer Frank Jay Haynes, who made the earliest winter photographs of the park, and scout Ed Wilson. Their twenty-nine day journey took them throughout the park.

Yellowstone National Park 🌲

Established in 1872 as the first National Park, Yellowstone is a region Indian tribes passed through, though only the Sheepeaters spent any significant amount of time there. Trappers also visited the region. John Colter likely passed through the southern end of the park in his explorations of 1806–1807, Jim Bridger was in the park and east of there along the Shoshone (Stinking Water) River, where he saw and reported on bubbling mud pots and other thermal features, giving that area the name Colter's Hell.

When established, the park quickly became a site for tourists to visit; in the early years they hunted and fished in the region. To establish some controls, the army established Fort Yellowstone (*see entry*). Later management was transferred to the Department of the Interior/National Park Service.

NOTES

1. At this time, Grant was in office as President of the United States.

2. Rans Baker, interview by the author, Rawlins, Wyoming, 12 September 2009.

3. Though Frémont and his companions could likely see Elk Mountain, which he called Medicine Butte, and the Sweetwater Range, even on the clearest day they would not have been able to view the Wind River mountain range from that vantage point.

4. This comes from Chief Joseph's surrender speech, published initially in the *Bismarck Tri-Weekly Herald*, and also in the official report by Col. Oliver O. Howard as well as by *Harper's Weekly*, November 17, 1877. The surrender speech was recorded by Howard's aide, Lieutenant C. E. S. Wood. It is likely these were not Joseph's actual words but rather were the interpretation of what he said as recorded by Wood. This general account is from Candy Moulton, 2006, *Chief Joseph Guardian of the People* (New York: Forge Books).

5. This is a report by the Lewis-Burt command.

6. Although almost all nineteenth century references to Caspar Collins spell his name with an "a," a census document recently uncovered indicates it may actually have been spelled with an "e" just as the city spells the name.

7. Lieutenant Brown report at Fort Halleck, June 1865, quoted in Louise Bruning Erb, Ann Bruning Brown, and Gilberta Bruning Hughes, 1989, *The Bridger Pass Overland Trail 1862–1869 Through Colorado and Wyoming and Cross Roads at the Rawlins–Baggs Stage Road in Wyoming* (Littleton, CO: ERBGEM), page 70.

8. Bridger was a mountain man and civilian scout. The rank of major, likely, was a courtesy.

BIBLIOGRAPHY

Alcorn, Gay Day. 1984. *Tough Country*. Saratoga, WY: Legacy Press.

An Indian Massacre. 1894. *Saratoga Sun* (March 22).

Badger-Doyle, Susan. 2001. *Journeys to the Land of Gold*. Helena, MT: Montana Historical Society.

Barnhart, William R. 1969. *The Early History of Carbon County, Wyoming*. Master's thesis, Department of History, University of Wyoming, Laramie.

Blevins, Winfred. 1989. *Roadside History of Yellowstone National Park*. Missoula, MT: Mountain Press.

Bliss, Edward. 1931. Denver to Salt Lake by Overland Stage in 1862. *The Colorado Magazine*, 5(September): 190–197.

Bourke, John G. 1891. Facsimile edition. *On the Border with Crook*. Lincoln, NE: University of Nebraska Press, Bison Books. Original edition, New York: Charles Scribner's Sons.

Bradley, Glenn Danford. 1960. *The Saga of the Pony Express*. Edited by Waddell F. Smith. San Francisco: Hesperia House.

Brown, Dee. 1962. *Fort Phil Kearny: An American Saga*. Lincoln, NE: University of Nebraska Press.

Brown, Joseph. 1980. *The Mormon Trek West*. Garden City, NY: Doubleday.

Brown, Larry. 1995. *The Hog Ranches of Wyoming: Liquor, Lust & Lies Under Sagebrush Skies*. Glendo, WY: High Plains Press.

Brown, Mark. 1969. *The Plainsmen of the Yellowstone: A History of the Yellowstone Basin*. Lincoln, NE: Bison Books.

Bruff, J. Goldsborough. 1949. *Gold Rush*. Edited by Georgia Willis Read and Ruth Gaines. New York: Columbia University Press.

Bryan, F. T. (Lieutenant). 1857. Report concerning his operations in locating a practicable road between Fort Riley to Bridger's Pass 1856, 35th Cong., 1st sess. Senate Executive Document, 11, serial 920. Quoted in *Annals of Wyoming*, 1945 (January), 17(1): 24–54.

Bryans, Bill. 1990. *Deer Creek: Frontiers Crossroad in Pre-Territorial Wyoming*. Glenrock, WY: Glenrock Historical Commission.

Burton, Sir Richard F. [1862] 1990. *The City of the Saints and Across the Rocky Mountains to California*. Niwot, CO: University Press of Colorado.

Carley, Maurine. 1956. Oregon Trail Trek No. 2, October 25, 1953. *Annals of Wyoming*, 28(1): 41–67.

————. 1957a. Oregon Trail Trek No. 4, September 26, 1954. *Annals of Wyoming*, 29(1): 67–85.

————. 1957b. Oregon Trail Trek No. 5, July 17, 1955. *Annals of Wyoming*, 29(2): 177–194.

————. 1961a. Overland Stage Trail—Trek No. 1, September 17, 1960. *Annals of Wyoming*, 33(1): 73–101.

————. 1961b. Overland Stage Trail—Trek No. 2, September 17, 1960. *Annals of Wyoming*, 33(2): 195–214.

————. 1970. The First Fifty Miles of the Oregon Trail in Wyoming— Trek No. 20, July 12–13, 1969. *Annals of Wyoming*, 42(1): 41–103.

Casement, J. S. 1868. Letter to his wife, Frances Casement, 1 August. Casement Collection, American Heritage Center, University of Wyoming, Laramie.

Champion, Nate. 1892. Journal. *Cheyenne Daily Leader*, 14 April and Chicago Herald, 16 April.

Chittenden, Hiram Martin. 1927. *The Yellowstone National Park*. 3rd ed. St. Paul, MN: J. E. Haynes.

Crutchfield, James A. 1993. *It Happened in Colorado*. Helena, MT: Falcon Press.

Cutting, A. Howard. Diary. Henry Huntington Library, San Marino, CA.

Davis, John W. 1993. *A Vast Amount of Ttrouble: A History of the Spring Creek Raid*. Niwot, CO: University of Colorado Press.

Di Certo, Joseph. 2002. *The Saga of the Pony Express*. Missoula, MT: Mountain Press.

Dilts, Fred, Jr. 1956. Talk given during Oregon Trail Trek No. 1, June 28, 1953. Reported in Maurine Carley, Oregon Trail Trek No. 2, October 25, 1953, *Annals of Wyoming*, 28(1): 41–67.

Doane, Robinson. 1928. Tales of the Dakota. *South Dakota Historical Collections*, XIV: 536.

Edwards, Glen R. 1956, April. Talk given during Oregon Trail Trek No. 1, June 28, 1953. Reported in Maurine Carley, Oregon Trail Trek No. 2, October 25, 1953, *Annals of Wyoming*, 28(1): 41–67.

Ellison, R. S. 1981. *Fort Bridger: A Brief History*. Cheyenne, WY: Wyoming State Archives, Museums and Historical Department.

Erb, Louise Bruning, Ann Bruning Brown, and Gilberta Bruning Hughes. 1989. *The Bridger Pass Overland Trail 1862–1869 Through Colorado and Wyoming and Cross Roads at the Rawlins–Baggs Stage Road in Wyoming*. Littleton, CO: ERBGEM.

Ferris, W. A. 1940. *Introduction to Life in the Rocky Mountains*. Denver, CO: Old West Publishing.

Fisher, S. G. 1877. Diary and correspondence (September 10). Idaho Historical Library.

Frazier, Robert W. 1972, *Forts of the West*. 2nd ed. Norman, OK: University of Oklahoma Press.

Frémont, John C. 1845. Report of the exploring expedition to the Rocky Mountains in the year 1842 and to Oregon and North California in the years 1843–44. 23rd Cong. [U. S. Senate document].

Goering, Dale. 1970. Rifle Pits and Nearby Points of Interest. In Maurine Carley, The First Fifty Miles of the Oregon Trail in Wyoming—Trek No. 20, July 12–13, 1969. *Annals of Wyoming*, 42(1): 77–103.

Goertz, Allen. 1970. Sand Point Stage and Pony Express Station. In Maurine Carley, The First Fifty Miles of the Oregon Trail in Wyoming—Trek No. 20, July 12–13, 1969. *Annals of Wyoming*, 42(1): 41–67.

Greene, Jerome A. 2003. *Morning Star Dawn: The Powder River Expedition and the Northern Cheyennes, 1876*. Norman, OK: University of Oklahoma Press.

Gunderson, Mary Alice. 1988. *Devils Tower: Stories in Stone*. Glendo, WY: High Plains Press.

Hafen, LeRoy. 1926. *The Overland Mail, 1849–1862*. Cleveland, OH: Arthur H. Clark.

———. 1930. Fraeb's Last Fight and How Battle Creek Got Its Name. *The Colorado Magazine* (May).

Hafen, LeRoy, and Ann W. Hafen. 1960. *Handcarts to Zion: The Story of a Unique Western Migration, 1856–1860*. Glendale, CA: Arthur H. Clark.

Haines, Aubrey L. 1981. *Historic Sites Along the Oregon Trail*. St. Louis, MO: Patrice Press.

Hebard, Grace R., and E. A. Brininstool. 1922. *The Bozeman Trail, Vol. 1*. Cleveland, OH: Arthur H. Clark.

Herr, Henry R. Diary. *Miscellaneous Overland Journeys to the Pacific*. Manuscript 1506, Oregon Historical Society, Portland, OR.

History of the Union Pacific Coal Mines. 1940. Omaha, NE: Colonial Press.

Homsher, Lola M. 1949. *The History of Albany County, WY to 1880*. Master's thesis, Department of History, University of Wyoming, Laramie.

Howard, O. O. 1881. *Nez Perce Joseph: An Account of His Ancestors, His Lands, His Confederates, His Enemies, His Murders, His War, His Pursuits and Capture*. Boston: Lee and Shephard.

Hufsmith, George W. 1993. *The Wyoming Lynching of Cattle Kate, 1889*. Glendo, WY: High Plains Press.

Hurd, Emilie. 1961. Big Pond Station. In Maurine Carley, Overland Stage Trail—Trek No. 2, September 17, 1960. *Annals of Wyoming*, 33(2): 195–214.

Huseas, Marion McMillan. 1991. *Sweetwater Gold: Wyoming's Gold Rush 1867–1871*. Cheyenne, WY: Corral of Westerners International.

Interview with E. N. Lewis. 1865. *Rocky Mountain News*. (August 16).

Irving, Washington. 1839. *Astoria; or, Enterprise Beyond the Rocky Mountains*. London: Richard Brantley.

Irving, Washington. 1873. *The Adventures of Captain Bonneville, U.S.A. in the Rocky Mountains and the Far West* (author's rev. ed.). Philadelphia: J. B. Lippincott.

Jackson, Donald, and Mary L. Spence, eds. 1970. *The Expeditions of John Charles Fremont. Vol. 1, Travels from 1833 to 1844*. Urbana, IL: University of Illinois Press.

Jackson, W. H. 1940. *Time Exposure*. New York: G. P. Putnam.

Jones, Robert Huhn. 2005. *Guarding the Overland Trails: The Eleventh Ohio Cavalry in the Civil War*. Spokane, WA: Arthur H. Clark.

Jording, Mike. 1992. *A Few Interested Residents: Wyoming Historical Markers and Monuments*. Helena, MT: Skyhouse.

Kime, Wayne R., ed. 1996. *The Black Hills Journals of Colonel Richard Irving Dodge*. Norman, OK: University of Oklahoma Press.

Larson, T. A. 1978. *History of Wyoming*. 2nd rev. ed. Lincoln, NE: University of Nebraska Press.

Letters of 1862 Reveal Indian Trouble Along the Overland Mail Route. 1943. *Annals of Wyoming*, 15(2): 150–152.

Ludlow, Fitzhugh. 1870. *Heart of the Continent*. New York: Hurd & Houghton.

Mattes, Merrill. 1960. *Indians, Infants, and Infantry*. Denver: Old West.

Mattison, Ray H. 1955. *Devils Tower: History and Culture—The First Fifty Years*. Available January 3, 2010, from http://www.nps.gov/deto/historyculture .

McFarling, Lloyd. 1955. A Trip to the Black Hills in 1876. *Annals of Wyoming*, 27(1): 35–42.

McGillycuddy, Julia B. 1941. *McGillycuddy, Agent*. Stanford, CA: Stanford University Press. [Reprinted as *Blood on the Moon*. 1990. Lincoln, NE: Bison Books, University of Nebraska Press.]

McGillycuddy, Valentine T. 1913. Letter to Walter Camp, 14 Jan. Camp Collection, Reel 1, Brigham Young University, Salt Lake City, UT.

Monnett, John H. 2008. *Where a Hundred Soldiers Were Killed: The Struggle for the Powder River Country in 1866 and the Making of the Fetterman Myth*. Albuquerque: University of New Mexico Press.

Morrison, W. W. 1971. Story of Little Mary Kelly (pp. 272–275). In Third Segment of the Oregon Trail: Douglas to Independence Rock, compiled by Maurine Carley. *Annals of Wyoming*, 43(2), 270–295.

Moulton, Candy. 1994. *Legacy of the Tetons: Homesteading in Grand Teton National Park*. Caldwell, ID: Tamarack Books.

Moulton, Candy. 1995. *Roadside History of Wyoming*. Missoula, MT: Mountain Press.

———. 2006. *Chief Joseph: Guardian of the People*. New York: Forge Books.

———— and Ben Kern. 1997. *Wagon Wheels: A Contemporary Journey on the Oregon Trail.* Glendo, WY: High Plains Press.

Murray, Robert A. 1968. *Military Posts in the Powder River Country of Wyoming, 1865–1894.* Lincoln, NE: University of Nebraska Press.

————. 1969. *The Army on the Powder River.* Bellevue, NE: Old Army Press.

National Archives & Records Administration. n.d. *Records Relating to Investigations of the Ft. Philip Kearney (or Fetterman) Massacre: Testimony of Col. Henry B. Carrington* (Page 1, M740 roll 1 of 1). Transcribed by Billy Markland. Available November 23, 2009, from http://freepages.history.rootsweb.ancestry.com/~familyinformation/fpk/car_1.html

Nesmith, James W. 1939. Diary of the Emigration of 1843. *Oregon Historical Quarterly* (September): 341.

Olson, James C. 1965. *Red Cloud and the Sioux Problem.* Lincoln, NE: University of Nebraska Press.

O'Neal, Bill. 2004. *The Johnson County War.* Austin, TX: Eakin Press.

Ordway, Edward. 1929. Reminiscences of Edward Ordway. *Annals of Wyoming,* 6(1 & 2): 169–188.

Paden, Irene. 1943. *The Wake of the Prairie Schooner.* New York: MacMillan.

Palmer, Joel. 1947. *Journal of Ttravels over the Rocky Mountains, to the Mouth of the Columbia River, Made During the Years 1845 and 1846.* Cincinnati, OH: J. A. & U. P. James.

Parker, Frank. 1895. Recollections of the Nez Perce War. *The Northwest* (July): 3–6.

Parkman, Francis. 1846. *The Oregon Trail.* Garden City, NY: Doubleday.

Patterson, Richard. 1998. *Butch Cassidy: A Biography.* Lincoln, NE: University of Nebraska Press.

Pennock, Isaac B. 1865. Diary of Isaac B. Pennick [*sic*], First Sergeant, Company T, Eleventh Kansas Cavalry. [Typed copy]. Wyoming State Archives, Henry Clay Bretney Collection C-1657, Folder 11.

Peryam, Edward Crevor. 1952. Interview. Encampment, WY. 16 September. Transcript at the Grand Encampment Museum, Encampment.

Richardson, Leander P. 1877. A Trip to the Black Hills. *Scribner's Monthly,* 13(6).

Riley, Glenda, and Richard Etulain, eds. 2003. *Wild Women of the Old West.* Golden, CO: Fulcrum.

Rosenberg, Robert G. 1989, February. *Military Context and Property Types.* Report for Wyoming State Historic Preservation Office, Cheyenne, WY.

Running the Gauntlet. 1892. *Saratoga Sun* (November 24).

Ryan, Gary David. 1963. Camp Walbach, Nebraska Territory, 1858–1859: The Military Post at Cheyenne Pass. *Annals of Wyoming*, 35(1).

Sage, Rufus. 1857. Rocky Mountain Life or, Startling Scenes and Perilous Adventures in the Far West During an Expedition of Three Years. Boston: Wentworth.

Scribner Buys Nuzum Out. 1903. *Saratoga Sun* (July 23): 1.

Settle, Raymond, and Mary Settle. 1955. *Saddles and Spurs: The Pony Express Saga.* Harrison, PA: Stackpole.

Shaw, J. C. 1926. Indian Story of Sylvester Sherman: Account of Burning of the Heck Reel Wagon Train. *Annals of Wyoming*, 3(3): 177–180.

Spring, Agnes Wright. 1927. *Caspar Collins.* New York: Columbia University Press.

———. 1948. *The Cheyenne and Black Hills Stage and Express Routes.* Lincoln, NE: University of Nebraska Press.

Strong Men, Brave Women, and Sturdy Children Crossed the Wilderness Afoot. 1914, January 4. *Salt Lake Tribune.*

Tanner, Russ. 1984. *Report—The Controversy Surrounding the Granger Stage Station, Wyoming.* Bureau of Land Management, Rock Springs, WY.

Tierney, Ed. 1961. LaClede Station. In Maurine Carley, Overland Stage Trail—Trek No. 2, September 17, 1960. *Annals of Wyoming*, 33(2): 210.

Treaty with the Sioux—Brulé, Oglala, Miniconjou, Yanktonai, Hunkpapa, Blackfeet, Cuthead, Two Kettle, Sans Arcs, and Santee— and Arapaho, 1868 (Treaty of Fort Laramie, 1868). In Charles J. Kappler, comp. and ed., 1904. *Indian Affairs: Laws and Treaties—Vol. II: Treaties* (pp. 998–1007). Washington, D.C.: Government Printing Office. Available April 15, 2010, from Oklahoma State University Library, Electronic Publishing Center: http://digital.library.okstate.edu/kappler/Vol2/treaties/sio0998.htm

Trenholm, Virginia Cole. 1964. *The Shoshonis: Sentinels of the Rockies*. Norman, OK: University of Oklahoma Press.

U. S. Congress. Senate. *Testimony as the Claim of Ben Holladay*. 46th Cong., 2nd sess., 1890. Senate Miscellaneous Document 19.

Urbanek, Mae. 1990. *Wyoming Place Names*. 2nd ed. Missoula, MT: Mountain Press.

Van Pelt, Lori. 2003. Cattle Kate, Homesteader or Cattle Thief. In *Wild Women of the Old West* (p. 159). Edited by Glenda Riley and Richard Etulain. Golden, CO: Fulcrum.

Vaughn, J. W. Vaughn, and L. C. Bishop. 1958. The Heck Reel Wagon Burning. *Annals of Wyoming*, 30(2).

Ward, J. O. 1927. Fort Fetterman. *Annals of Wyoming*, 4(3): 357–364.

Wight, Jeremy. 1993. *Frederick W. Lander and the Lander Trail*. Bedford, WY: Star Valley Llama.

Wilfong, Cheryl. 1990. *Following the Nez Perce Trail*. 3rd ed. Corvallis, OR: Oregon State University.

Williams, Thomas. 1858. Letter to Acting Assistant Adjutant General, Headquarters, District of the Platte, 23 September. Letters Sent, Camp Walbach. Records of Army Commands, RG 9, National Archives, Washington, DC.

Winter, Zita. 1961. Dug Springs. In Maurine Carley, Overland Stage Trail—Trek No. 2, September 17, 1960. *Annals of Wyoming*, 33(2): 195–214.

Wyoming Recreation Commission. 1988. *Wyoming: A Guide to Historic Sites*. Basin, WY: Bighorn Publishers.

INDEX

Candy Moulton has written a dozen Western history books, including the Western Writers of America Spur Award winning *Chief
Joseph: Guardian of the People*, published by Forge Books.

As a journalist, Moulton edits the WWA *Roundup Magazine* and
the Oregon-California Trails Association *News From the Plains*. She
is a contributing editor for *True West* magazine and writes for *Persim-
mon Hill, American Cowboy, Wild West*, and several local and region-
al magazines and newspapers.

She is an executive producer for filmmaker Boston Productions
Inc. She wrote and produced *In Pursuit of a Dream,* a film for the
Oregon-California Trails Association, which won the Spur Award for
Best Documentary in 2010 from WWA. She co-wrote *Footsteps to
the West,* the orientation film for the National Historic Trails Interp-
retive Center in Casper, WY, which was a Spur Award Finalist as
Best Western Documentary in 2003.

Moulton works out of her home office on a ranch near Encampment, Wyoming. She holds a BS in journalism from the University
of Wyoming.

∾ NOTES ON THE PRODUCTION OF THE BOOK ∾

This book was simultaneously released in two editions.

A *limited edition* of only 200 copies was Smyth sewn
with headbands of blue and white,
bound in Traildust cloth, embossed with matte navy foil,
and wrapped in a full-color dustjacket.
Each copy is hand-numbered and signed by the author.

The *softcover trade edition* is covered with twelve-point stock,
printed in four colors, and coated with a scuff-free matte finish.

The text of both editions is from the Garamond Family by Adobe.
Display type is LFH Antique Shop
and Post Antiqua by Adobe.
Icons, ornaments, and map symbols are from various foundries.

The book is printed on fifty-five pound Nature's Natural,
an acid-free, recycled paper
by Thomson-Shore.